Growing Up Resilient

Ways to Build Resilience
in Children and Youth

ankin
anlou

camh
Centre for Addiction and Mental Health
Centre de toxicomanie et de santé mentale

Growing Up Resilient: Ways to Build Resilience in Children and Youth

Library and Archives Canada Cataloguing in Publication
Barankin, Tatyana
Growing up resilient : ways to build resilience in children and youth / Tatyana Barankin, Nazilla Khanlou.

Includes bibliographical references.
ISBN: 978-0-88868-504-9 (PRINT)
ISBN: 978-0-88868-592-6 (PDF)
ISBN: 978-0-88868-593-3 (HTML)

I. Resilience (Personality trait) in children.
II. Resilience (Personality trait) in adolescence.
III. Adaptability (Psychology) in children.
IV. Mental health promotion.
V. Family—Mental health. I. Khanlou, Nazilla, date. II. Title.

BF723.R46B37 2007   155.4'1824   C2006-904859-2

Printed in Canada
© 2007 Centre for Addiction and Mental Health

For information on other CAMH publications or to place an order,
please contact:
Sales and Distribution
Tel.: 1 800 661-1111 or 416 595-6059 in Toronto
E-mail: publications@camh.net
Website: www.camh.net

This book was produced by:
DEVELOPMENT: Margaret Kittel Canale, CAMH
EDITORIAL: Diana Ballon, CAMH; Sharon Kirsch
ILLUSTRATIONS: Sandy Nichols
DESIGN: Anja Kessler, CAMH
PRINT PRODUCTION: Christine Harris, CAMH

P5601/2887/08-07

Contents

About the authors v

Acknowledgments vi

1 **The power of resilience** 1
   Approaching resilience 3
   Current thinking and practice 5
   About the book 5

2 **Understanding resilience** 7
   Resilience 9
   Mental health 10
   Mental health promotion 10
   Mental health problems and resilience 11
   Risk and protective factors 11
   The development of resilience 14

3 **Enhancing resilience: Individual factors** 17
   Developmental transitions 19
   Key individual factors affecting resilience 21
      Temperament 21
      Learning strengths 24
      Feelings and emotions 27
      Self-concept 31
      Ways of thinking 33

Adaptive skills 35
Social skills 37
Physical health 39
Summary 43

4 Enhancing resilience: Family factors **45**
The importance of family 47
Key family factors affecting resilience 48
Attachment 49
Communication 50
Family structure 54
Parent relations 56
Parenting style 58
Sibling relations 61
Parents' health 62
Support outside the family 63
Summary 65

5 Enhancing resilience: Environmental factors **67**
Social determinants of resilience 69
Key environmental factors affecting resilience 70
Inclusion: Having a sense of belonging 71
Social conditions: Society promoting resilience 74
Access: Systems promoting resilience 78
Involvement: Youth's participation in the world around them . . .82
Summary 84

Glossary **87**

References **91**

Resources **95**

About the authors

This book arose out of an interdisciplinary collaboration. Its authors are mental health professionals whose research, education and practice are in the field of child and youth mental health promotion and treatment.

Tatyana Barankin, MD, FRCPC, DCP

Dr. Tatyana Barankin is a staff psychiatrist in the Child, Youth and Family Program at the Centre for Addiction and Mental Health and staff psychiatrist at Toronto's Hospital for Sick Children. She is an associate professor and Head of Continuing Medical Education, Child and Adolescent Division, in the Department of Psychiatry at the University of Toronto.

Dr. Barankin graduated from medical school in St. Petersburg, Russia (formerly Leningrad, Soviet Union) and then specialized in pediatrics. She completed her psychiatric training at the University of Toronto, sub-specializing in child psychiatry. Her main areas of work include mood and anxiety disorders across the life spectrum, school psychiatry, preventive interventions in populations at risk, and gender and cultural aspects of mental health problems. Dr. Barankin teaches medical students, residents and community physicians in the Child, Youth and Family Program at CAMH. She has also been a consultant to community agencies, the Toronto District School Board and French boards of education. Dr. Barankin has won numerous awards for her leadership and knowledge dissemination in Continuing Medical Education and was quoted as an opinion leader in Time magazine. To balance her professional life, she devotes time to her family and friends, and to her hobbies, music and art.

Nazilla Khanlou, RN, PhD

Dr. Nazilla Khanlou is an associate professor at the Faculty of Nursing and Department of Psychiatry at the University of Toronto. Her graduate work includes an MSc in community health from the University of Toronto and a PhD in clinical health sciences from McMaster University in Hamilton. Her clinical background is in psychiatric nursing. Dr. Khanlou's research is in the interdisciplinary field of community-based mental health promotion, focusing on youth and women in multicultural and urban settings where immigrants settle. Her research focuses on youth self-concept, particularly as it relates to cultural identity and self-esteem; gendered post-migration resettlement experiences; and participatory mental health promotion.

Dr. Khanlou teaches at undergraduate and graduate levels and provides student super-vision. She has received many academic awards—most recently, a Mentorship

Award from the Centre for Equity in Health and Society. Dr. Khanlou is the Health Domain Leader of the Centre of Excellence for Research on Immigration and Settlement (CERIS) in Toronto and was a visiting scholar (2005–2006) at the Wellesley Urban Health Institute. She is a member of the University of Toronto's Social Justice Cluster and the Faculty of Nursing's Diversities and Politics of Health Research Cluster. Dr. Khanlou has published articles and reports on immigrant youth and women, and mental health. She speaks fluent Farsi and Azari.

Dr. Khanlou also devotes herself to family, friends and community participation. She writes poetry, and enjoys walks in nature and travelling.

Acknowledgments

We acknowledge and thank the many people who contributed *to Growing Up Resilient*. Dr. Mark Sanford, a former CAMH colleague, receives special thanks for significant contributions he made in earlier stages of the book's development. We are also grateful to the parents, teachers, health care providers, scientific experts and health promoters who reviewed earlier drafts of this book.

Project manager
Margaret Kittel Canale, MEd, CAMH

Writers
Margaret Kittel Canale, MEd, CAMH
Karen Shenfeld, BA

Reviewers
Amanda Bender, intensive therapist, Child & Youth Wellness Centre of Leeds and Grenville; Robyn B. Dewar, parent; Dr. Jackie Eldridge, EdD, assistant professor, Faculty of Education, University of Ontario: Institute of Technology; Shona M. Fraser, poet activist and mother; Lindsay Gallagher, BA, addiction counsellor/intake worker, Addiction Services of Thames Valley; Sandra Hamilton, child and youth counsellor, Madame Vanier Children's Services; Colleen Kelly, MSW, RSW, family therapist, CAMH; Mary-Lee Konnry, BA, BEd, MEd, school administrator, teacher and counsellor, York Catholic District School Board; Daintry Topshee, co-ordinator, Frederick Banting Alternate Site, Ottawa-Carleton District School Board

1

The power of resilience

1

Approaching resilience

What enables some young people to do well in school, to form meaningful relationships and feel hopeful about the future, in spite of adversity, while others become depressed or self-destructive? This is a question that is often asked—by researchers, clinicians, parents, teachers and young people themselves. And it was a question that was raised through Dr. Tatyana Barankin's own clinical practice.

In 1989, Dr. Barankin founded and directed a clinic in Toronto for children at risk for developing mental health problems—the only clinic of its kind in Canada. Over the next 15 years, she—as head of a team—assessed and treated close to 700 families—all of whom had at least one parent with a mental health problem. While she saw many people overwhelmed by the challenges in their lives, she also saw other family members who managed extremely well, and who had an almost supernormal way of coping. The adversity in their lives varied: some had experienced abuse, others had a parent with a severe mental health problem, some had gone through teen pregnancy, still others had been injured in car accidents or had come to Canada seeking refuge from war in their home country. But they all had one thing in common: these young people managed not only to adapt, but to blossom—in spite of the trauma they had experienced. Through individual, sibling and group cognitive therapy, these children and families became more adaptable in dealing with family stress.

Dr. Nazilla Khanlou's experience was a natural complement to Dr. Barankin's. Like Dr. Barankin, she has an understanding of clinical issues (having worked as a psychiatric nurse on an acute inpatient psychiatric unit). As well, she has a community perspective—having, over the last decade, shifted her focus toward mental health promotion among youth in community settings such as schools.

Dr. Khanlou became interested in resilience after doing a study among girls whose parents had immigrated to Canada. While going through transitions associated with adolescence, she saw how the young women in the study were able to straddle their cultures of origin and Canadian mainstream culture, were active in school and their communities and were positive about their future.

Since then, she has conducted other studies that have, like her first study, revealed a profound strength and resilience in youth. Her findings differ from the one-dimensional way youth are often perceived in contemporary society, which is as a "problem" requiring a solution, rather than as young people with strengths, creativity and contributions to make. Dr. Khanlou believes this book will help to change this image by encouraging parents, teachers and front-line workers to focus on young people's strengths, and by making them more aware and understanding of the difficulties in young people's lives. She also believes that we need to address prejudice and discrimination in our society, because inclusive and just environments help all people thrive and reach their potential.

The combination of a clinical and community background has impressed on Dr. Khanlou how promoting mental health and resilience in children and youth requires multiple approaches. Differing approaches are needed not only in improving health and social services, but also in challenging society to look at the social determinants of mental health (such as income, education and inclusion) and their influence on young people. In the last chapter, on environmental factors, she wants to make the reader more aware of how social factors affect young people's sense of well-being—and how resilience in children and youth is a result of the interplay between their individual traits and abilities and the social context in which they live.

Dr. Barankin and Dr. Khanlou draw from diverse fields—such as psychology, psychiatry, nursing, sociology and health promotion—to provide a new way of looking at resilience in children and youth. Their message is hopeful—that is, that most children are resilient and that resilience is something that can be developed and nurtured.

Current thinking and practice

Resilience is not a new term in academic and prevention circles, nor is the idea of nurturing people's strengths a new idea. In fact, the view that resilience is an important aspect of mental well-being has been gaining attention among health professionals and researchers over the last 25 or so years. Their experience and studies have increasingly shown that how people cope with the challenges they face in different life stages is influenced by their sense of who they are, how they relate to the world and others around them, and how well they manage the various parts of their lives.

However, there is little written for parents, teachers and front-line workers about the qualities that help make young people resilient. The resilience literature has tended to focus on the individual, whereas we see resilience as requiring a more ecological, integrative approach that looks at the interactions between young people and their families, communities and society. We wanted to write a book especially for parents, and for the people who work or volunteer with young people each day—from teachers and school administrators to daycare, recreation-centre and youth-shelter workers; sports coaches; Girl Guide and Boy Scout leaders; camp counsellors and directors. By exploring the interplay of factors that contribute to resilience, we hope that front-line workers, teachers and parents will be better equipped to nurture resilience in the young people in their lives.

About the book

Growing Up Resilient explains what health care providers mean when they talk about resilience. It explores what risk and protective factors can affect resilience in young people. And it gives tips on how to build resilience in children and youth.

We have divided the factors that affect resilience into three broad categories: those that relate to the individual, the family and the environment or community within which the young person lives. This division not only helps parents, teachers, community workers and others more clearly understand the roots of resilience—it also enables them to use a variety of ways to build resilience in children and youth. Young people's individual, family and environmental factors are interrelated, complex and diverse—and there is more than one way to help young people become resilient.

Each chapter is introduced by the story of a real person from around the world who, as a child or adolescent, lived through extremely difficult circumstances. These stories are meant to inspire us—to remind us how some people not only manage to adapt but actually excel in the face of life's difficulties. Their achievements are remarkable because they showcase how their resilience benefited not only themselves, but also the world around them.

Many of us know people who may not be famous, but who have also shown great strength and resilience in their lives. They may be our parents, friends or neighbours. Or they may be us. The potential for resilience lives in everyone.

Note: Readers may be unfamiliar with some of the words used in this book. Wherever possible, we have defined more complicated words and ideas as they come up in the text. We have also provided a glossary on page 87.

2

Understanding resilience

PERSONAL STORY OF RESILIENCE

Kim Phuc Phan Thi was immortalized in a news photograph showing her as a nine-year-old girl, burned by a napalm bomb, screaming and running naked down a road away from her burning village in Vietnam on June 8, 1972, during the Vietnam War.

The photographer who took the Pulitzer Prize–winning picture immediately took her and other family members to a hospital. Several of Kim Phuc's family members, including two younger brothers, died from their injuries. Kim Phuc spent many painful months in hospital receiving treatment for third-degree burns that covered more than half her body. Her mother stayed with her to help her through the trauma. Over the years, Phuc had 17 operations. The photographer continued to visit her until he left Vietnam three years later. He brought her books and other gifts and set up a donation fund for her family. He kept in touch with her and saw her again when she was an adult.

Phuc returned to her village about two years after the bombings that burned her. In her late teens, she enrolled in pre-medical studies, because she wanted to be like the doctors who saved her life. But in 1982, the Vietnamese government took her out of school because they wanted to use her and her fame as a national icon of the war. The government eventually agreed to allow Phuc to go to Cuba to continue her medical studies. In Cuba, Phuc met the man she would marry.

Today Kim Phuc lives in Canada with her husband and children. (She and her husband were flying from Cuba to Moscow on their honeymoon in 1992 when they defected to Canada on a refuelling stop in Gander, Newfoundland.)

Kim Phuc credits her religious beliefs with giving her much-needed strength in her life. She is an advocate for peace who speaks of forgiveness. Kim Phuc was named a UNESCO Goodwill Ambassador in 1997. She was awarded the Order of Ontario in 2004. And she started the Kim Foundation to provide medical and psychological help for children affected by war. In a 1996 Veterans' Day speech at the United States Vietnam War Memorial, Phuc said "[W]e cannot change history but we should try to do good things for the present and for the future to promote peace." Kim Phuc is a vivid example of the power of human resilience. ☙

2

To understand how to nurture resilience in children and youth, we need to first understand its link to mental health and mental health promotion. The following are key concepts used in the book.

Resilience

Resilience involves being able to recover from difficulties or change—to function as well as before and then move forward. Many refer to this as "bouncing back" from difficulties or challenges.

People who are resilient can effectively cope with, or adapt to, stress and challenging life situations. They learn from the experience of being able to effectively manage in one situation, making them better able to cope with stresses and challenges in future situations. In other words, dealing with challenges can make us grow and can make us stronger. Rather than merely bouncing back, we're better prepared than we were before to face challenges that lie ahead.

Resilient children tend to be empathic; that is, they can understand and sympathize with the feelings of others. They tend to be good communicators who are able to solve problems. They have a strong interest in school, and are dedicated to learning. They're driven to achieve goals. They're involved in meaningful activities. They're hopeful about the future. They have a solid relationship with one or more adults. And they live in safe and well-functioning families and communities.

Mental health

Part of being resilient is having good mental health. *Mental health* involves balancing the different aspects of life: the physical, intellectual, social, emotional and spiritual. It involves our ability to think, feel, act and interact in a way that we can enjoy our lives and cope with the challenges that arise. Mental health also involves how we think about and appraise ourselves, our lives and the people we know and care about. It involves our ability to make realistic sense of—and react meaningfully to—the world around us. It affects our ability to make choices and decisions.

Mental health promotion

As its name suggests, mental health promotion is about promoting mental health. Promoting mental health encourages the development of resilience. The reverse is also true: promoting resilience leads to better mental health. In fact, resilience is a central concept within the mental health promotion framework. According to the Centre for Health Promotion (1997), mental health promotion (MHP) improves the ability of people and the communities they live in "to take control over their lives and improve their mental health." MHP strategies nurture individuals and families and the communities they live in; build on their strengths; provide them with opportunities; create safe spaces for them; and support each to become resilient. More specifically, MHP strategies encourage cultural sensitivity and awareness, together with respect for people's differences, regardless of their age, gender, sexual orientation, culture, socio-economic situation or abilities.

MHP benefits everyone in his or her everyday life—whether the person is healthy; is at risk for developing difficulties (such as a substance use problem); or has an existing health problem (such as depression). That's because MHP is a holistic, or ecological, approach to health that focuses on the physical, mental, emotional and spiritual well-being of individuals, families and communities. And it does so in ways that create environments that are respectful to everyone and that enhance people's capacity to adapt and grow from challenges.

In using this book to take steps to building resilience in the children and youth in your life, you will also be involved in the exciting arena of mental health promotion.

Mental health problems and resilience

Can a resilient child or youth develop a mental health problem? And, conversely, can a young person with a mental health problem be resilient? The answer to both of these questions is yes. Not all health problems are avoidable, and even the most resilient young people can have mental health problems, such as anxiety or problems with aggression. Furthermore, being resilient does not guarantee that young people will always have happy and productive lives.

One in five children in Canada has a mental health problem. These problems can show up in different ways. Children may be frequently sad, anxious or rebellious; have difficulty paying attention; have problems eating, sleeping or getting along with school-mates; or they may skip school. As adolescents, they may use alcohol or other drugs.

While these difficulties can lower a person's resilience, there are many things that can be done to help improve their resilience, as outlined in the tips listed at the end of each section on individual, family and environmental factors. These tips are strategies that parents, teachers and front-line workers can use in their interactions with young people: they are not meant to address more challenging issues that may require the help of a trained health care provider.

Risk and protective factors

Mental health professionals speak about risk and protective factors as the key to under-standing resilience. *Risk and protective factors* are characteristics of individuals, their families and their communities or environments that either increase (protective factors) or decrease (risk factors) the likelihood that a young person will be resilient. In essence, protective factors help to protect children and youth from the negative effects of risk factors.

Human beings are complicated. For example, there likely isn't a simple reason as to why one person (or even one sibling) will be resilient, and another not so resilient, even though they are both brought up under the same circumstances.

Risk and protective factors do not occur in a vacuum, nor do they exist independently of one another. Young people's resilience is determined by the interplay of individual characteristics, the characteristics of the families within which they live, and the characteristics of their physical and social environments. For example, living with both parents is considered a protective factor for children and youth; however, if one parent is abusive to the child or to the other parent, then living with that parent could be a risk factor and not living with that parent could be a protective factor.

The tables of protective and risk factors presented at the end of chapters 3, 4 and 5 might give the impression that they are opposite sides of the same characteristic, and that they carry the same weight in a young person's life. Fortunately that's not the case. Even though there may be risk factors or challenges in young people's lives that cannot be changed, protective factors can be fostered or nurtured (if they're not already there) to help children and youth adapt and function better and become more resilient.

We can't always foresee how resilient someone will be based solely on risk and protective factors, because no formula exists for predicting human behaviour. What may be a risk factor for one child may be a protective factor for another. And what may be a risk factor for one youth in one situation or at one time may be a protective factor for the same youth in other situations or at other times.

For example, young people sometimes take on parental roles when the parent has a mental health or substance use problem. The challenge—of being confronted with adult problems, of having to take care of themselves, of having to take care of a parent, and of being denied a normal childhood—will be a risk factor for some young people who struggle to cope with roles they are not ready for. For other young people, however, taking on adult responsibilities may develop in them the ability to multi-task, organize, problem-solve and make decisions.

Some young people with many risk factors will be resilient. Other young people with many protective factors might not manage as well. For example, some youth live in troubled family situations in neighbourhoods where the sale of illegal drugs and other crimes are common. Yet they still manage to help raise brothers and sisters, make good friends, graduate from high school and contribute to their communities. Still other youth have loving parents and live in safe, well-resourced communities yet have low self-esteem and develop behavioural problems that compromise their resilience. Even within the same family, one child may be resilient while others are not.

Studies indicate that risk and protective factors are usually cumulative: the more protective factors in young people's lives, and the fewer risk factors, the greater the probability that these children or youth will be resilient. The reverse is also true: the more risk factors and the fewer protective factors in young people's lives, the greater the likelihood that they will not be resilient and will develop a range of problems. These problems can include failure at school, aggressive and criminal behaviour, injuring themselves or others, substance use problems and mental health problems.

The good news is that introducing even a few protective factors can shift the balance and help many children and youth flourish. For example, for young people growing up in families with low incomes, and with little money to pay for extra-curricular activities, the building of a neighbourhood recreation centre offering free or low-cost activities could serve as a protective factor. So could the launching of a youth choir or an amateur-theatre program in a small town or rural church.

The development of resilience

Young people are like trees. They come in various shapes and sizes and grow up in most parts of the world. Families can be thought of as the soil and water at the base of trees. Schools, neighbourhoods, communities and society at large can be compared to the sun, rainfall, insects, birds and animals. The different characteristics of trees, qualities of soils and weather conditions (such as the amount of sun and rainfall) can affect the health and growth of trees. In a similar way, the varying traits of young people, and the characteristics of their families and environments, can positively or negatively affect young people's health and growth.

Trees go through developmental stages as they mature from young saplings to full-grown specimens. Children also go through developmental stages on their way to adulthood, and what happens to them at various stages of development can affect their outcomes. Resilient children and youth grow, branch out and flower when systems supporting their healthy development (such as well-functioning families and environments) work together. Such young people are more likely to withstand and overcome challenges, learn from them, and develop and succeed in healthy ways.

No one can guarantee children and youth lives free from challenges. All young people need protective factors to help cushion them from problems they may encounter. Caring and socially responsible adults (such as parents, family members, neighbours, daycare workers, teachers and other school staff, spiritual leaders, health care providers, social service providers, police, storekeepers and coaches) can support and facilitate young people's resilience.

In the following chapters, we discuss ways to strengthen individuals, families and environments to build resilience in children and youth. We present ways to reduce the presence and impact of risk factors but put more emphasis on how to create and build protective factors that will nurture young people's strengths. We recognize that resilience is a complex concept and that we need to include multiple ways of promoting it.

Resilient children can be encouraged to become more resilient. And children who seem to have less resilience can be helped to develop it.

3

Enhancing resilience:
Individual factors

PERSONAL STORY OF RESILIENCE

Elie Wiesel was born in 1928 in a small town in Transylvania (now part of Romania) into a close-knit Jewish family.

The security of his childhood ended abruptly with World War II and the arrival of the Nazis in 1944. At age 15, he was sent to Auschwitz concentration camp in Poland, where he was separated from his mother and sisters. For the next year, he and his father were starved, beaten and shuttled from camp to camp on foot or in open cattle cars without food, proper shoes or clothing. In the last months of the war, Wiesel's father died of dysentery, starvation, exhaustion and exposure.

Elie Wiesel managed to survive. After the war, he found asylum in France, where he learned that his two older sisters had also survived the war. He mastered French, studied philosophy at the Sorbonne and became a journalist. In the 1950s he wrote two memoirs about his disturbing experiences.

Wiesel has authored more than 35 works dealing with Judaism, the Holocaust and the moral responsibility of people to stand up against hatred, racism and genocide. He has used his fame to plead for justice for oppressed peoples around the world. In 1985 he was awarded the U.S. Congressional Medal of Freedom and, in 1986, the Nobel Peace Prize.

Elie Wiesel not only survived but also rose above the unspeakable horrors of his wartime experience. He did so by demonstrating a strength of will, intelligence and compassion, and fortified by memories of a close-knit family and strong ties to his cultural community. Some of these qualities he may have been born with; others he undoubtedly developed. They are protective factors associated with resilience. ⌘

3

Developmental transitions

From birth through to adulthood, children and youth experience change regularly—and, for the most part, it is change over which they have little control.

Childhood and adolescence are marked by developmental transitions or life stages. Young people undergo countless—often monumental—physical, emotional and intellectual changes. They begin their social lives by forming attachments to their families and primary caregivers, then move on to socialize with others at daycare, at school, on sports teams, at spiritual gatherings and in the broader community.

Resilient children and youth master various tasks as they progress from birth to adulthood. In the infancy to preschool years, they form a strong, secure attachment to the people who care for them; they learn to speak; they develop self-control; and they follow instructions. In the middle childhood years, they adapt to the school environment; they get along well with schoolmates; and they further develop behaviour that shows they accept and follow society's expectations, rules and laws.

Adolescence—the transition from childhood to adulthood—can be a particularly challenging time for young people. Adolescents undergo the physical changes of puberty. They slowly begin to take on adult responsibilities by furthering their education and by getting part-time jobs. Healthy, resilient adolescents manage to cope with the challenges of this developmental stage. They navigate intense emotions—of romantic love and rejection—and strong sexual feelings and pressures to experiment with alcohol and other drugs. Through these experiences, they emerge as healthy adults who continue to successfully manage change and demanding circumstances.

Many children and youth must also adapt to additional demands and stresses. Some, for example, are born with or develop physical disabilities that may affect their ability to see, move or learn new things. Others live in families with low incomes, in homes where one or both parents have substance use problems, in homes where there is violence, or in unsafe neighbourhoods.

Although the media portrays adolescence as a period of tremendous upheaval, stress and conflict, most teens succeed at school, are attached to their families and communities, do not develop problems with alcohol or other drugs, and do not engage in violent or criminal behaviour. And, despite occasional protests, most need and want adults to be part of their lives, recognizing that adults can nurture, teach, guide and protect them on their journey to adulthood.

How young people manage these developmental stages varies. There may be times of transition when young people are more adversely affected by risk factors than at other times. The age at which children and youth are exposed to particular risk or protective factors can also affect how they respond to them. For example, infants may be protected from particular stresses, such as parents' separation or divorce, because of their limited understanding of what is going on around them. Older children may likewise be unaffected by the same stresses if they are helped by an adult to understand and adapt, or if they know how to separate themselves emotionally (that is, if they know who they are as an individual and have strong boundaries). For example, children who have a parent with a physical or mental health problem may care deeply about the parent yet understand that it is not their problem, that they did not cause it and that they cannot solve it.

Parents, teachers and other supportive adults can help children and youth successfully make the transition from one developmental stage to the next. Knowing the normal stages of child development will help them not expect too much or too little of young people.

Libraries contain many good books on child development to help adults know what is reasonable to ask of the young people in their lives. (*For examples, please see "Resources" on page 95.*) High but realistic expectations, along with positive messages, can help build resilience.

Key individual factors affecting resilience

Everyone has individual factors that help make them who they are and determine their levels of resilience. We have divided these individual factors into the following eight categories:

- temperament
- learning strengths
- feelings and emotions
- self-concept
- ways of thinking
- adaptive skills
- social skills
- physical health.

The nature and effects of these individual factors can and do change over time, depending on how young people interact with family, friends, their community and the world around them. Understanding how each of these factors contributes to young people's resilience will help the adults in their lives create effective strategies to reduce young people's risk factors and build on protective ones.

Temperament

Relaxed. Undemanding. Good-natured. Sociable. These are the traits of an easygoing temperament. Temperament refers to a combination of inborn and acquired characteristics that influence how people relate to others around them, and how they respond to different situations.

Characteristics related to temperament include the person's activity level, ability to adapt, mood, attention span, persistence and the intensity of his or her reactions. Depending on the combination of these (and other individual) characteristics, a young person may have an easy or difficult temperament, a "slow to warm up" temperament or a disorganized temperament.

About 40 per cent of children have an easy temperament: they adapt well to change and, in most situations, have a positive mood. A much smaller percentage fit into the other categories previously mentioned. Children with a difficult temperament tend to be withdrawn; adapt slowly to change; and often express intense, negative emotions. Children with a slow-to-warm-up temperament are similar to children with a difficult temperament, in that they tend to be withdrawn or shy and have difficulty adapting to change; however, their emotional reactions tend to be less intense and they are more likely to develop anxiety problems. Children with a disorganized temperament vary in their responses, making it hard to predict how they will react emotionally.

While children's inborn temperament is apparent in the first year of life, their temperament can and will be affected by their environment. For example, infants and children who are treated with warmth, caring and sensitivity are more likely to be resilient, well-adapted children and youth—regardless of the characteristics they were born with. While temperament is not the same as personality, it is one of the significant factors in its development.

RESILIENCE-BUILDING TIPS

◆ Learn to recognize differences in young people's temperaments, so that you can help them to adapt to new situations and so that you can respond to each person based on his or her own unique needs, abilities and skills.

◆ Be aware of and sensitive to young people's temperaments. For example, if a young person has a reactive, overly excitable temperament, recognize the need to act calmly or keep the young person away from excessive stimulation.

◆ Help young people to be more aware of how their feelings affect their social and emotional development. For example, teachers can structure lessons to help students learn about feelings: what evokes them and how feelings affect relationships with others. To develop this skill, teachers could ask students to include descriptions of emotions in their essays and journals: people who are positive, friendly and reach out to others attract more friends; people who are angry appear unfriendly or threatening and others tend to avoid them.

◆ Help young people acquire skills that will offset more difficult temperaments, such as impatience or a quick temper.

◆ Model and teach social skills that help young people get along well with others.

◆ Direct young people who might need special help to counsellors who offer social skills training programs. (*For a discussion of social skills, see page 37.*)

◆ When children misbehave, let them know that while you may not approve of their behaviour, you still care about them and believe in them.

◆ Provide a "cooling off" time for young people with a difficult temperament. If they have intense reactions, for example, you could introduce them slowly to new and possibly overwhelmingly situations, so they have time to get used to the change. You could also schedule regular intervals of calm or quiet activities to prevent them from having overpowering feelings.

◆ Gradually and sensitively expose children with a shy temperament to social groups. Encourage them to nurture friendships and have playmates by, for example, setting up play dates with other children.

◆ Provide children with a disorganized temperament with a predictable, consistent environment.

Learning strengths

Highly intelligent. Good problem-solving skills. Eager to learn new things. Able to plan, critique and seek help from others. Creative. Imaginative. Flexible. Curious. Motivated. Goal-oriented. Possessing a strong sense of purpose. Good student. These are the qualities of people with well-developed learning skills. Because they have more experiences of success, they have greater self-esteem and overall resilience.

Learning strengths refers to ways in which children and youth take in, absorb and apply information. Young people's learning strengths are a combination of their inborn intelligence and the knowledge and skills they develop through formal and informal education. In other words, they can increase their learning abilities, regardless of the intelligence they are born with. "Intelligence" includes memory and the ability to find creative solutions to problems, and even to find humour in difficult circumstances.

From birth, infants observe and absorb the world around them. By listening and interacting with others, infants begin to develop language skills even before they speak. From age nine months to five years, children develop thinking skills that help them learn to read and do mathematics.

Informal learning at home and in the community contributes to a young person's learning strengths. Children benefit from being exposed to a range of stimulating and challenging learning environments. For instance, they learn through structured and unstructured play, by exploring the natural environment, and by meeting people from different backgrounds.

As children enter preschool and progress to the higher grades, the school system becomes another important source of learning. Teachers that engage the support of parents and have firm but fair rules with high academic standards are likely to produce students committed to learning. *(For a more complete discussion of schools that build resilience, see page 78.)*

Teachers can give students opportunities to raise issues that are bothering them and help them learn how to make decisions and find solutions on their own. They can also teach them how to speak up in responsible and socially acceptable ways. For instance, they can model respectful ways of speaking, by never screaming or belittling students and by listening when students express ideas. Young people need to know that their voices are heard.

Adolescents, in particular, tend to make quick decisions that can lead to their getting involved in risky behaviours, such as drinking and driving. As adults, we can help adolescents learn to weigh their options and consider consequences and outcomes. Doing so may help them learn how to make their own decisions, without being influenced or pressured by friends.

Children and youth's learning strengths vary. We can support young people's individual talents and interests, and celebrate their accomplishments, be they physical or artistic. We can accept their limitations, while helping them to not judge themselves too harshly. And we can help them set goals based on a realistic understanding of their abilities and interests, rather than on other people's expectations.

By being exposed to various learning environments, young people develop awareness, imagination, know-how and initiative. They learn how to handle a variety of social situations and interact with different kinds of people. They are challenged to handle problems, learn from the experience and continue to grow. They develop the ability to come up with more than one solution to solving a problem. They also learn to think about past negative experiences in ways that allow them to define the experience and move beyond it. In other words, they develop resilience.

RESILIENCE-BUILDING TIPS

For infants and toddlers

❖ Provide infants with stimulating and varied experiences that are appropriate for their age—such as singing songs, reciting rhymes, smiling, putting mobiles over their cribs, and giving them rattles and other toys.

❖ Offer young children a special place in the home and at daycare where they can play freely with various toys and props that encourage spontaneity and imagination.

❖ Give toddlers opportunities to climb and run in public parks, scribble on paper, play with blocks and have fun with other children. Opportunities to play can help toddlers develop the physical skills, concentration, and social and language skills that they will need to be ready for school.

For young children and adolescents

◆ Read to younger children, help them with their homework, take them to libraries and museums, and encourage adolescents to go on their own. (Some museums, science centres and art galleries are free at certain times or offer price-reduced family tickets.)

◆ Encourage children to take part in science fairs, chess competitions, spelling bees, sports and, if financially and otherwise possible, send them to day and overnight camps that teach different skills.

◆ Help young people to channel their physical energy; for instance, by taking them to swim classes or to sports activities at a community centre or by jogging with them in a park.

◆ Teach young children decision-making skills by allowing them to make simple decisions, such as deciding what to wear. Parents can ask, for example: "Would you like to wear the blue shirt or the green shirt today?" "The navy pants or the black pants?" Pay attention and notice early on if young people are struggling with basic developmental tasks—such as speaking, reading, writing or arithmetic. If they are, arrange as soon as possible for special help for them in and out of school.

◆ Teach children and youth the steps to solve a problem—such as defining the problem, thinking up alternative solutions, choosing the best solution, carrying out the solution and then considering the outcome. For instance, if the child gets a low grade in school, his parent could encourage him to discuss his difficulties with the teacher, and learn how he could improve.

◆ Nurture decision-making skills by giving students opportunities to make decisions as a group. For example, students could decide where to go for a class trip. Teachers could encourage them to first brainstorm ideas, and then consider each of the idea's pros and cons.

◆ Encourage children to pursue activities that interest them, without concern for whether those activities are usually done by girls or boys. For example, support and encourage boys to cook, sew or dance and girls to program computers and repair cars if those are the activities that they appear to be excited about.

◆ Offer extra attention to children with learning disabilities. For example, teachers can introduce special methods and curricula into the classroom that will help them succeed; the school or community centre can organize a tutoring program for extra help; and the young people themselves can be encouraged to develop skills in sports, arts and other areas of ability in order to feel good about themselves.

Feelings and emotions

Are calm, caring and happy. React respectfully to other people's emotions. Openly express their emotions. Are able to control their anger and get over frustrations quickly. Can keep things in perspective. Are able to be comforted when they're upset. Use humour to cope. Are empathic (that is, they are able to understand and sympathize with someone's feelings and motives). People with these qualities are more resilient than those without them.

Experiencing and expressing emotions is part of life. However, young people's emotional experiences and their ability to manage specific emotions vary greatly. How young people express their emotions and react to other people's emotions are determined by tendencies they are born with and by their early life experiences. Research shows that, between birth and age two, children learn a lot about how to control their anger and other emotional states.

Parents and caregivers who respond lovingly to infants' emotions—whether these are emotions of joy (such as smiling and laughing) or emotions of distress (such as crying)—help them develop control over how they express their emotions. Infants who are comforted by those around them are then better able to comfort or soothe themselves. And children who know they can rely on their caregivers feel secure, are more trusting and experience less stress.

Families who talk about how they feel help young people learn to identify their own feelings and communicate them to others. The ability to label their feelings helps young people consider what is happening around them and allows them to make decisions about how to deal effectively with their feelings. Boys and girls often express feelings and emotions differently. Boys tend to act out or externalize emotions, sometimes by being aggressive or abusing alcohol or other drugs. Girls, on the other hand, tend to internalize their feelings and emotions, or keep them to themselves, making them more vulnerable to depression. Increasingly, however, some girls are engaging in aggressive and risky behaviours, such as bullying, gang membership, and alcohol and other drug use.

Young people imitate the behaviours of adults. As adults, we must therefore look at how we handle our own emotions and stresses. Are we able to control our feelings of anger? Are we overwhelmed by feelings of anxiety or depression?

Children and youth who are able to handle a range of emotions have learned how to use emotional support well, use problem-solving methods to figure out the underlying sources of emotions, and distract themselves with "positive activities," such as listening to music. Seeing themselves successfully managing a difficult emotion in one situation helps young people realize they can successfully manage that same emotion should it arise in another situation. The experience also helps them avoid relying on negative coping strategies, such as drinking or using other substances. Managing difficult emotions builds resilience.

RESILIENCE-BUILDING TIPS

Expressing feelings

◈ Encourage young people to express their feelings, and then respond respectfully to the child's feelings. Emphasize that experiencing a range of emotions—whether pain, fear, anger or anxiety—is human, but that we don't need to act out these emotions (for example, by getting angry in a way that is hurtful).

◈ Help young people become aware that expressing some of their feelings may be destructive to themselves and to others: for example, feelings that reflect racist attitudes and other forms of prejudice.

◈ Help young people to see how communicating their feelings to someone who is sensitive (that is, someone whom they trust and feel understands them) can make a positive difference in their lives. For instance, if a child tells his mother that he is sad that she doesn't go to watch his soccer games, then she has the chance to make amends by arranging to see future games.

◈ Consider the young people's age and developmental stage and their capacity to respond to a situation when helping young people deal with their emotional states. For example, when children are very young, distracting them with enjoyable activities can be helpful. However, as they get older, parents might want to help the child explore and express painful feelings: for example, parents could share how they coped with a difficult situation, so that the child feels less isolated and can learn how to master his or her own problems.

Being empathic

◈ Pay close attention to young people's words and actions so as not to underestimate the emotion they are feeling or overestimate their ability to cope. For example, if a child is scared of a monster in the dark, listen to the child's emotions and fears instead of simply telling him there's nothing to fear.

◈ Teach empathy by talking young people through their feelings. For example, a teacher could ask someone who has been bullying another child how he thinks that child whom he has bullied might feel. The teacher could also ask: "How would you feel if someone said bad things about you?"

Coping with sadness or anxiety

◆ Listen carefully and talk young people through situations to help them develop skills to handle future stress. When children and youth express sad thoughts to a sensitive adult, for example, they can get the support they need to heal.

◆ Show young people relaxation techniques (for example, breathing exercises) to help reduce their anxiety.

◆ Teach young people to use the word "I," rather than "you," when they are upset with someone. For example, instead of someone accusing the other person of failing to do something, or putting that person down with comments such as, "You are so inconsiderate. You never meet me on time," suggest something more helpful, such as "I feel hurt and upset when we have an agreement to meet and you show up late."

Dealing with anger and conflict

◆ Get help for children and youth who have difficulty controlling their tempers. Through anger management training, offered through a parenting centre or mental health agency, young people can learn simple techniques to control the physical reactions that anger causes as well as the intensity of their angry feelings.

◆ Model ways to debate and resolve conflicts. Get help for yourself if you need it. If you lose control of your temper, talk about your feelings and apologize if your behaviour was inappropriate.

◆ Model ways to teach young people how to replace angry thoughts with calmer and more rational ones. (For example, rather than the child saying, "I hate my friend. I'm never going to talk to her again. I'm going to get back at her," he could be encouraged to say, "I am frustrated with my friend right now.

It's understandable that I'm upset with her. But it's not the end of the world, and getting angry is not going to help."

Self-concept

Confident. Optimistic about the future. Realistic about their abilities. Able to use self-discipline. Able to cope with criticism and solve their own problems. Feel a sense of belonging to their family or community. These are the signs of someone with a positive self-concept.

Young people's self-esteem (how they judge their worth) is tied, in part, to their self-concept. Thoughts such as, "I feel good about myself," "I am as good as my peers in school" or "I am a good hockey player" show positive self-esteem.

Young people's self-concept is also tied to their identity (how they see themselves in different roles and relationships). Thoughts such as, "I am a young girl," "I am First Nations," "I am a high-school student" or "I am gay" relate to identity. Young people's identities are based on how they view themselves—for example, in terms of gender, sexual orientation, culture or roles (as an athlete, student or musician) and how they think others view and label them.

People may be born with a positive self-concept, but more likely, we develop or strengthen this concept of ourselves over time as a result of the positive messages and influences of our family and environment. As noted in the following chapter (*see page 49*), infants develop attachments to the adults who take care of them. Children flourish when they know that the important adults in their lives care about them, express interest in what they do, and appreciate and accept them for who they are.

A young person's self-concept may vary over time and in different situations. Young people may, for example, feel self-confident and accepted at home, but not around the neighbourhood or at school. They may feel accepted and liked one moment and then alone and unpopular the next.

Adolescence, in particular, is a time when young people try out various identities to find the ones that fit them best. It's also a time when they try to discover their own sense of uniqueness. We can help young people by reassuring them that we support and accept them, even during times when they feel others do not. We can also help young people think about and possibly challenge expected roles and stereotypes by discussing how such ideas limit people's choices. (For example, if we discover children or youth excluding or picking on a classmate who has lesbian parents, we can discuss with them the importance and value of having two loving, supportive parents, regardless of their gender.)

Feeling good about ourselves comes more easily when we grow up in a society that accepts and appreciates us the way we are and want to be. Such a social environment embraces a wide range of roles, values, beliefs and ideas. Chapter 5 (*page 69*) presents many ways that we can work to build such an environment—an environment in which children and youth feel free to express and be proud of their unique cultural and other identities.

A positive self-concept contributes to resilience. The more positive young people's self-concept (and related self-esteem and sense of identity), the more likely they will be able to deal with life's stresses and challenges.

RESILIENCE-BUILDING TIPS

◈ Create opportunities for young people to develop a positive self-concept. For example, praise them for their accomplishments, listen attentively, take an interest in what they are doing and let them know that their contributions are valuable. This way, they develop their own sense of self, rather than merely learning to act in a way that will elicit approval.

◈ Help children and youth handle defeats, rather than focusing on the importance of constant success.

◈ Let young people know that your love and support remain unchanged, particularly when they feel unsupported by others, or when they're going through a crisis or feeling disappointed. When the crisis has passed, help them reflect constructively on what went wrong. Tell them that the next time they go through a hard time, they'll be able to use knowledge gained from over-coming past difficulties to help them make it through.

❖ Encourage young people to get involved with various activities (such as sports, music lessons and volunteer work) in which they will gain skills that enhance the way they feel about them-selves.

❖ Encourage teens to face problems or situations that threaten their self-concept—such as taking an exam or breaking up with a boyfriend or girlfriend. Support them by role-playing a diffi-cult conversation or by providing information and resources.

❖ Model positive attitudes about yourselves, and show that you can manage your own struggles. This includes avoiding mak-ing negative comments about yourselves, such as "I look fat" or "I can't do this."

❖ If a child is showing significant stress, he or she could be referred to a mental health agency where a multidisciplinary team (made up of a social worker, a psychologist, a psychia-trist, a nurse and possibly a special education teacher) could rule out certain problems and develop an accurate idea of the child's problem.

Ways of thinking

Think positively. Are optimistic. Look forward to the future. Recognize the need to work hard to accomplish things. Young people with these attributes tend to be resilient.

We all think silently or talk to ourselves. (Our silent thinking, or self-talk, reflects our unspoken attitudes, expectations and beliefs.) We also use self-talk to problem-solve, manage our inner conflicts, plan for the future and regulate our emotional reactions. Silent thinking is mostly positive or mostly negative, depending on our self-concept.

The degree to which young people think positively is affected by their temperament, as well as by their life situations and their interactions with family, friends, teachers and other adults. We cannot hear young people's silent inner dialogue but, by being attuned and empathic, we can help young people become aware of their negative thoughts and negative views of themselves and replace them with more realistic, positive thoughts.

Of course, positive thinking can never replace hard work: a young person cannot pass a test, play piano or make a school team without studying, practising or training. To find contentment, young people also need to develop a realistic view of themselves and their abilities.

As many sports psychologists and business leaders know, positive thinking can reduce stress, improve performance and increase optimism. Research links optimism to fewer mental health problems (such as depression) and better life outcomes. Supportive families and environments can also enhance positive thinking. (*To learn more about positive thinking, refer to Seligman's book* The Optimistic Child *listed in "Resources" on page 96.*)

RESILIENCE-BUILDING TIPS

◈ Counter children's negative thinking with other, more encouraging ways of seeing their situation. For example, a child afraid of failing an exam she has studied hard for could be encouraged to tell herself: "I have studied hard, and I know the material well. I am smart enough to succeed."

◈ Be as optimistic as possible about your own future, while making sure that your optimism is grounded in reality.

◈ Provide young people with a range of possibilities and goals that they can choose from, work toward, look forward to and realistically achieve.

◈ Let young people know that failure is acceptable and sometimes unavoidable and that they can move on or perhaps try again.

◈ Expose young people to positive news. An overexposure to doom-and-gloom newscasts can negatively affect sensitive children and adolescents.

◈ Help young people set positive goals and maintain self-discipline to see projects through to the end.

◈ Suggest that youth read self-help books, available in libraries and bookstores, which address ways of thinking positively. (*See "Resources" on page 95 for ideas.*)

◈ Arrange for a child or youth who is depressed or anxious to get a proper assessment at a mental health agency. One form of therapy that can be helpful is cognitive-behavioural therapy (CBT). Through CBT, people learn how their thinking patterns, which may have been developed in the past to deal with difficult or painful experiences, can be identified and changed in their day-to-day lives.

Adaptive skills

Persevere through difficulties. Able to problem-solve; make decisions; resolve conflicts; choose practical, realistic solutions; and manage stress. Know how to reach out for help. Are flexible when negotiating with others. People with these kinds of *adaptive skills* will be prepared to successfully manage the difficulties and challenges in their lives.

As noted earlier in this chapter, all young people face problems, stresses and challenges throughout their childhood and adolescent years. Young people develop skills through the support of others. We can help children and youth learn how to look realistically at their situation and set appropriate goals. We can guide them so they learn how to judge when it's reasonable to persevere at attaining a goal, or when it may be wiser to be flexible and choose another course or option.

Young people need to learn how to solve problems and make decisions as part of a group as well as on their own. At the same time, they should also know that they can turn to other people for support, whether this means getting advice from parents or being able to talk to a grandparent, another extended family member or family friend. There are times when children and youth may need someone to intervene on their behalf. For example, two students could agree on a teacher to help them resolve a conflict—or, in a more serious example, an involved adult could remove a child or youth from an unhealthy family or school situation and refer him or her to appropriate education, health and social services.

RESILIENCE-BUILDING TIPS

◆ Help young people develop their problem-solving and decision-making skills. (*See "Learning Strengths" on page 24.*) Emphasize that problem solving is a skill that develops over time and with practice, and involves a series of steps. For example, when young people face a problem or issue, help them identify a positive outcome, search for alternatives to reach the outcome, and select the best alternative to reach their goal.

◆ Help children and youth anticipate and plan how they will deal with difficulties, so they have an easier time overcoming challenges.

◆ Make young people aware of various coping strategies. If one thing doesn't work for them, help them discover that they can find something else that does. For instance, if a qualified student can't afford to go away to university, perhaps he or she could live at home and apply for a scholarship.

◆ Encourage young people to do simple, pleasurable activities to reduce stress and relax, such as listening to their favourite music, playing with a pet, taking up a sport or hobby, or going for a walk or run.

◆ Suggest ways that young people can take part in volunteer work, sports or other team-building activities where they can practise working with people; learn when to handle issues on their own; and when to ask others for help.

◈ Encourage young people to develop a sense of competence based on their talents and abilities.

◈ Encourage young people to develop supportive relationships with peers, coaches, clergy or others who can be a positive influence. Having such friendships can help young people to be more adaptable, because friendships have a positive affect on our mental health. Friendships make us feel valued, give us someone to share with and confide in, give us encouragement and support, and offer us role models—in short, friendships allow people to function at their best.

Social skills

Able to listen to, and understand, the ideas and intentions of others. Affectionate. Assertive. Caring. Empathic. Helpful. Self-confident. Sense of humour. Able to solve conflicts peacefully and communicate ideas and feelings in a considerate manner. Able to stand up for themselves. These are qualities of people with good *social skills.* Having good social skills is positively associated with resilience.

Social skills reflect the ways in which children and youth co-operate and interact with others. They also reflect the way young people make friends, and the kinds of people they make friends with. Adequate peer relationships in childhood are one of the best predictors of good mental health in adulthood.

Infants interact with others from the moment they are born. They learn socially accepted behaviour from watching others (such as parents, grandparents and other extended family members) and copying their behaviour. Good social skills develop best in a home where family members are loving and respectful, where they provide opportunities for role-modelling along with positive feedback, opportunities for making choices and decisions, and clearly defined boundaries and rules.

Boundaries ensure children's right to privacy, protect them from intrusion and allow them to develop assertiveness. Conversely, violating young people's boundaries (for example, by looking through their diaries and other possessions, or by barging in on their discussions with their friends on the phone) hurts their sense of trust and sense of separateness.

As children are exposed to more and more people and situations, such as at daycare or preschool, they have more opportunities to learn how to negotiate and co-operate. Children who learn to solve or cope with minor disagreements are better prepared to manage and cope with bigger conflicts as they get older.

We are more likely to cultivate social skills through our experiences than to be born with them. And while we may be born with a tendency to certain traits, such as shyness or aggression, caregivers, teachers and other important people in our lives can help guide and support us to get along well with our peers.

Well-developed social skills will serve young people well as they move out into their community, whether playing team sports, interacting with staff in the local convenience store, or becoming the next prime minister.

RESILIENCE-BUILDING TIPS

❖ Help young people learn basic social skills. Teach them how to greet others when they meet them, to say please and thank you, to ask permission when they want something, to learn how to start conversations, to take their turn, to listen during conversations, to apologize when necessary and to be respectful.

❖ Encourage children and youth to consider what effect their behaviour has on others and to consider how others think and feel in social situations.

❖ Teach young people how to communicate their feelings, ideas and opinions without displaying anger or putting down others.

❖ Enrol children and youth who have difficulty getting along with others in conflict-resolution programs. These programs— offered through mental health agencies and by private counsellors—teach people how to come up with possible solutions to a conflict by identifying their feelings and understanding what they want, the deeper reasons underlying what they want and feel, and the views of others involved in the conflict. (*See* Greene's The Explosive Child *in "Resources" on page 96.*)

◆ Model good social skills and positive behaviour, such as caring, respect and tact. Young people can learn these skills from what they observe. They are then more likely to choose friends who also share these skills.

◆ Create opportunities for friends to visit. This gives parents natural ways to model social skills for their children, as well as opportunities for their children to interact with others. Teachers can use the same strategy with classroom visitors.

◆ Help young people develop conversational skills. Talk with them, so they learn how to express their thoughts and feelings and find out how other people express their thoughts and feelings.

◆ Encourage children and youth to be assertive as opposed to reacting with aggression or being a pushover.

Physical health

Well nourished. Fit, active and energetic. Not surprisingly, people who are physically healthy are more likely to be resilient, and to have good mental health, than people with serious medical problems or disabilities. However, not all illness is avoidable and even the most resilient people can become sick.

Young people who are intelligent, have a particular talent or have good supports are often able to use these attributes to compensate for poor health. For instance, they may be able to maintain good friendships and keep doing certain non-physical activities, in spite of their illness. But it will be more difficult for them to be resilient than it is for healthy children. Building resilience in young people involves preventing illness, as well as reducing the overall impact of health problems in a person's life.

Parents can influence their children's health. This can start even before the baby is born. For example, pregnant women are more likely to have healthy babies if they eat a variety of nutritious foods; keep physically fit; and do not smoke cigarettes, drink alcohol or use other drugs.

In the early years (from birth to age two), one of parents' main concerns is to keep babies and toddlers safe: to avoid them becoming dehydrated; to prevent children from being injured by a fall; and to monitor what they eat to reduce the risk of allergic reactions, choking or poisoning. Nutritious foods are also important: breastfeeding when possible (to boost the immune system) and feeding babies organic food if possible. Other things parents can do to enhance the health of their children include taking them to the doctor for well-baby checkups and immunizations, and ensuring that baby car seats are correctly installed.

As children get older, parents need to ensure that children wear bike helmets, and are properly fastened into car seats. Children also need to be encouraged to eat a variety of healthy foods, to exercise regularly and to have a proper sleep routine. As they get older and are ready to be sexually active, youth need to be encouraged to follow safer sexual practices. (Lack of physical activity, obesity and sexually transmitted infections are major concerns in today's youth.)

At any point in childhood, the risk of a serious and painful medical illness, such as cancer, poses added challenges. Asthma, diabetes, epilepsy, cancer and repeated hospitalizations are other conditions that have a great impact on children and youth's emotional and social world. How young people adapt to physical health problems varies greatly. Some thrive, despite ongoing illness or disability, while others become quite despairing. Young people will need the support of their families (including siblings), friends and the community to cope with a range of feelings, such as anxiety, fear and the effects of trauma. This support is particularly important at stressful times: for example, when a child has to undergo painful procedures or be hospitalized, which often involves being separated from parents.

RESILIENCE-BUILDING TIPS

◈ Encourage young people to get exercise, whether this means biking, walking, swimming, dancing or other sports. At the same time, limit the amount of television they are allowed to watch.

◈ Nurture realistic optimism in children and youth who are ill or in poor health by building on their strengths. You can do this by encouraging them to get involved in activities they will enjoy and can succeed in.

◈ Provide young people with a wide variety of fresh, nourishing foods, including five to 10 servings of fruit and vegetables per day.

◈ Make sure that children and youth see a family doctor and dentist for regular checkups.

◈ Model good health yourself, by getting exercise, eating well, not smoking and drinking in moderation.

◈ Protect young children by taking reasonable safety precautions—for example, by putting up baby gates at the tops and bottoms of stairs, and by putting children in car seats (or seat belts when they get older).

◈ Provide older children and youth with guidance so they participate more safely in physical activities—such as ensuring they wear a helmet when biking, or suggesting they take lessons before engaging in potentially dangerous activities, such as rock climbing or kayaking on rapids.

◈ Stick up for and support young people who are being left out or picked on by other students or adults. (Young people who are obese or have other physical disabilities—including visual or hearing problems—are more likely to be ostracized, making it harder for them to cope, make friends and feel confident.)

◈ Provide young people with education around sexually transmitted illnesses.

◈ Advocate for healthy physical environments, such as clean air, nutritious food and safe roads.

◈ Advocate for daily physical education classes in schools.

For young people who have health problems

◈ Help them to understand the nature of their illness and available treatments.

◈ Make sure that parents, grandparents or other important people are available for younger children who have to be in hospital.

◈ Ensure that their education is not interrupted while they are sick.

◈ Ensure that they continue to have contact with their friends.

Summary

Individual factors affecting the resilience of children and youth

PROTECTIVE FACTORS	RISK FACTORS
○ good adaptive skills	○ genetic vulnerability to substance use or mental health problems
○ easygoing temperament	
○ sense of humour	○ physical health problems
○ ability to adapt	○ low self-esteem
○ problem-solving and decision-making skills	○ learning or other disability
	○ poor nutrition
○ social skills	○ academic failure
○ communication skills	○ difficult temperament
○ assertiveness	○ poor impulse control
○ empathy	○ unsafe physical environments (for example, pollution, violence)
○ high intelligence	
○ optimism: sense of hope, purpose and direction	○ hearing and visual disabilities
○ involvement in helping others	
○ ability to resolve conflicts	
○ good health	
○ talents and creativity	
○ flexible thinking	
○ self-discipline	
○ hobbies and interests	

4

Enhancing resilience:
Family factors

PERSONAL STORY OF RESILIENCE

In 1880, in a small town in Alabama, Helen Keller was born a healthy, happy baby. But less than two years later, she suddenly came down with a high fever, leaving her blind, deaf and unable to speak.

Helen's frustration led her to scream and throw violent temper tantrums. Many of her relatives regarded her as a wild animal. Her parents, however, never gave up on her. After searching for someone to help her, they met Anne Sullivan, her now-famous teacher.

With Anne's help, Helen Keller learned to speak not only English, but French, German, Greek and Latin. She graduated from Radcliffe College (now part of Harvard University) and later became a world-famous speaker and author of 11 books. Helen Keller's mission to champion the rights of the sensorially handicapped altered our view of people with disabilities and remapped the boundaries of sight and sense. Despite being blind, deaf and mute, she had many qualities that helped foster her resilience and protect her from the effects of her disabilities: she had a supportive teacher and loving parents, who had unshakable faith in Helen and who worked tirelessly to get her the help that she needed. ⍖

4

In this chapter, we focus on how the family helps to build resilience in children and youth.

Families vary in terms of the challenges they face, the internal and external resources available to them, and how well they respond to difficulties. Challenges can range from a serious illness to a family member's death to financial hardship, imprisonment or migration. Internal resources can be a close-knit family, good problem solving and clear boundaries, while external resources can be a supportive community, extended family and affiliation with a religious or spiritual institution. In other words, families as a unit have a resilience level of their own, which is more than the sum of the individual members' resilience. The way in which families respond to challenges varies over time, across situations and according to their belief systems.

The importance of family

Resilient families function effectively: family members have strong bonds, show affection, support one another, are flexible when they need to be, and share a commitment to work through the challenges they face together. They also comfort one another, encourage the sharing of feelings and find pleasure (and even humorous moments) through challenging times. Resilient families tend to be optimistic.

A well-functioning family is a protective factor that keeps young people grounded and helps them flourish and grow. Families that do not provide their children with appropriate encouragement and support create an obstacle to their developing resilience. However, many young people from poorly functioning families can and do develop into resilient adults because of their individual strengths, a caring relationship with a parent or other supportive adult, or community supports that allow them to thrive.

The term "family" does not just refer to people who are biologically related. It includes people you normally think of as family, such as parents, brothers and sisters, aunts and uncles, cousins and grandparents. And it can include caregivers, friends and neighbours. These are the people who take care of children and youth, protect them, nurture them, encourage them, support them, love them, guide them, teach them values and help them solve conflicts. They are the people who help young people develop the necessary skills to thrive.

Healthy, well-functioning families provide many of the elements young people need to succeed in life: love, acceptance, stability, a safe home environment, nutritious food, effective communication, guidance and support. Children need to know they can count on their families to be there for them no matter what difficulties arise. Families can provide them with this sense of belonging and security by creating recurring experiences and events that young people can expect and depend on, such as regular bedtime routines; and predictable dinner times, curfews and family celebrations (such as birthdays, religious and secular holidays, and cultural traditions). Families also need to provide children with opportunities for play and personal growth.

Key family factors affecting resilience

In the following sections, we focus on key family-related factors that contribute to the resilience of children and youth:

- attachment
- communication
- family structure
- parent relations

- parenting style
- sibling relations
- parents' health
- support outside the family.

Each of these factors is interrelated to the others, as well as to individual and environmental factors, to establish young people's resilience.

Attachment

Secure attachment generally refers to the relationship of trust that forms between infants and parents or care-givers. Infants with a secure attachment feel confident that the people who look after them will satisfy their needs and keep them safe. A secure attachment to a parent or caregiver early in life gives children a solid foundation for developing trust, self-esteem, self-control and confidence; for learning how to comfort themselves; and for forming healthy relationships with others. This

kind of healthy attachment reduces feelings of anxiety; for example, children learning to walk can feel comfortable exploring their environments, knowing that they can reach out for a supportive hand if necessary.

To be resilient, young people need a strong, positive emotional attachment to a caring, loving adult throughout childhood and adolescence. If a parent is unable to fill this role, other significant adults in young people's lives (such as a grandparent, extended family member or family friend) could provide them with the attention, guidance and support they need.

RESILIENCE-BUILDING TIPS

The following strategies are intended specifically for parents

◆ Pay attention to how your baby is communicating what he or she needs, and respond warmly to these needs (for example, by hugging, rocking, talking softly).

◆ Enlist another caring adult to support and provide guidance for your children, if one or more family members are unable to care for and spend time with your children over an extended period.

◆ Enrol in parenting classes to learn ways to strengthen your interactions with your children.

◆ Contact a parent hotline or speak to your doctor if you are feeling depressed; for instance, if you find that you aren't enjoying your baby, if you feel continually angry or overwhelmed with your child, or if parenting is bringing up painful memories from your own childhood.

Communication

Communication is the process by which information is exchanged between individuals. How well information is exchanged and understood among family members sets the tone for family interaction and plays a role in each of the family factors outlined in this book. Communication can be spoken or non-spoken. It can be empty or full of emotion. It can invite or discourage more communication.

Good communication involves all family members talking regularly to each other about their feelings and concerns and about what's happening in their lives. Family members listen to each other and care about how other members are feeling. They trust and accept each other's feelings, beliefs and points of view. And they respond to challenges by solving problems and conflicts together.

Communicating with parents can be an especially important factor for young people who are newcomers to Canada and who have the added challenge of adjusting to a new environment, a new language and new ways of doing things. Children need to feel that the family is a secure base whose strength they can draw on while adjusting.

Good communication does not mean young people must be informed of every detail about what goes on between other family members. How parents share information and what they share will depend on the stage of development of the children, as well as on parents' personal and cultural norms as they relate to talking about their feelings, determining what is appropriate and what they want to keep private.

Even when in conflict with teens over rules, chores, homework and peers, parents can emphasize the positive, rather than being critical of what their children are doing wrong. Teens need to know that though their parents may be unhappy with their behaviour, they still care, love and respect them as people.

Adolescence is the stage of life when many young people begin to experience romantic love and rejection, and strong sexual feelings. Some will begin to experiment with sex and start smoking, drinking alcohol and taking other drugs. Adolescents need our guidance to cope successfully with these challenges. Though parents may naturally find some subjects (such as dating and sexuality) difficult to discuss with adolescent children, they will still need to be open and direct when talking to them. This includes parents discussing their own values and beliefs, offering advice and warning their children about potentially unhealthy situations.

Research has shown that many teens do not listen and respond well to parents who simply tell them, without any discussion, "Don't do that." Telling teens not to do something will often not prevent them from becoming involved in risky behaviours, such as experimenting with illegal drugs. Teens are more willing to keep away from risky behaviours when parents take the time and energy to discuss the pros and cons of various behaviours with them, so that they can come to their own decisions. Ultimately young people will have to use their own judgment, take personal responsibility for their actions and make their own choices. Communicating well with family members is one of the best ways to ensure young people will make good choices.

Using abusive language or swear words, being excessively critical or speaking angrily to (or in front of) children can be harmful to them. Parents who speak this way can negatively affect relationships within the family and young people's healthy development. Communicating calmly and controlling one's emotions can be difficult, especially when parents may be trying to cope with their own stresses and problems or when their children are acting in ways they disapprove of. *(See the discussion of anger management training and family therapy in the tips that follow for ways to cope with these difficulties.)* Parents will need to be prepared to manage their own feelings if their teens make choices they don't agree with.

Some parents and teens who are having difficulties together may benefit from family therapy. Family therapy focuses on changing the way families interact. It aims to increase understanding and improve communication among family members, without placing the blame for problems on any one person. Counsellors who do family therapy often play a neutral role, making sure all family members get their say in a matter, while helping them sort through comments, issues and feelings. Counsellors may also model ways that family members can develop better skills to get their points across.

RESILIENCE-BUILDING TIPS

◈ Listen with interest when young people talk about their day-to-day lives, joys, problems and concerns. Listen even when you disagree, and express your willingness to talk about any subject and provide comfort and assurance. Be honest and focus on the positive. If a young person makes a joke or comment that is offensive or insulting, explain what his or her joke or comment is really expressing (for example, how the comment puts down others).

◈ Appreciate children and youth for their interests and efforts, rather than simply praising them. (For example, if a young boy has done a drawing, you could ask him to describe what's in the picture, and why he used certain colours.) Responding with flattery (praise that is exaggerated or not sincere) is more likely to result in the child repeating certain behaviours to get your attention, without developing his or her self-confidence.

◆ Model good communication by speaking in a way that is respectful and honest and that acknowledges the strengths of the person you are speaking to.

◆ Ask open-ended questions that require more than a "yes" or "no" response.

◆ Avoid "why" questions, as they tend to put young people on the defensive.

◆ Calmly discuss the process by which you arrived at an important decision.

◆ Discuss moral questions that arise in the daily news.

◆ Engage teens with non-threatening questions.

◆ Provide teens with developmentally appropriate information about sexual behaviours, sexual orientation and safer sex (for example, by encouraging teens to help protect themselves from disease and prevent unwanted pregnancies by using condoms).

◆ Work with a counsellor to learn anger management skills, if you are having difficulty controlling your temper around young people. Counsellors can teach you how to recognize and control the physical reactions that anger causes and to control the intensity of angry thoughts. They can also teach ways to keep your words and body language neutral and your voice level low, even when feeling frustrated or angry.

The following strategies are intended specifically for parents

◆ Define your own codes, standards and expectations to your children, and let them know, in advance, what consequences they will face if they do not follow them.

◈ Consider family therapy, if you are having difficulty communicating with your children.

◈ Encourage family communication by setting up informal, weekly family meetings. At such meetings, the family can plan their week, freely discuss any current or upcoming issues and talk through problems as a unit. Family meetings can provide young people with opportunities to learn how to plan their time, budget money, make decisions, and solve issues with other family members.

Family structure

Families are increasingly taking different forms. While traditionally, young people in Canada have been raised by a mom and dad who are married, children are increasingly raised by parents living common law, gay or lesbian parents, adoptive parents, foster parents, single parents and grandparents. If parents are separated or divorced, children may live with one parent, or move back and forth between parents in a shared custody arrangement; or, if mom or dad remarries, they may live with a step-parent in a blended family. If both parents remarry, children may move back and forth between two blended family households. Regardless of the structure of the family, the crucial factor determining resilience is that children feel that they have consistently supportive and nurturing adults in their lives. (*See "Attachment" on page 49.*)

As well as becoming more diverse, Canadian families are also getting smaller—with one or two children being the norm—while extended family households (with not only parents and children, but others, such as grandparents, aunts and uncles all living under the same roof) are decreasing. Extended family members have traditionally given added emotional and financial support to parents and children. With the extended family now disappearing, nuclear families are drawing increasingly on support from friends and the community. *(For more information, see "Support Outside the Family" on page 61 and Chapter 5, "Enhancing Resilience: Environmental Factors.")*

Regardless of form, each family faces its own challenges. Some experience loss due to the parents' separation or divorce or the death of a loved one. Some families with low incomes struggle to pay for basic needs, such as food and shelter. Some may live in neighbourhoods with a lot of noise, crime, pollution or lack of social services. Still other families may feel that they don't fit into the community where they're living if they are different from most of their neighbours (such as newcomers, or gay or lesbian parents). Others may have family members who have physical or mental health problems. And parents without partners may find it difficult to balance work and personal time because they don't have the support of another adult in raising their children.

Newcomer families to Canada face additional challenges. They may have left loved ones behind. They may experience financial challenges because the parents' educational and work experience are not fully recognized in Canada. And they may experience the reversal of roles between parents and children if the children speak better English or French than their parents. Refugees, in particular, may struggle from the sadness of knowing that they might never be able to return home, even for a visit. They may have experienced violence in their home country. Because of their experiences, some may have difficulty sleeping or have frequent nightmares.

While many changes to the family structure can create stress, positive outcomes that contribute to resilience are often just as likely. In a divorce situation, for example, young people may develop a stronger relationship with one or both parents and, depending on the circumstances, separation or divorce may remove young people from an abusive parent. Regardless of the type of structure, children and youth who have close bonds with their families are emotionally healthier, perform better in school and engage in fewer high-risk activities (such as substance use).

RESILIENCE-BUILDING TIPS

❖ Involve children and youth in mentoring programs, such as Big Brothers and Big Sisters, if they do not have significant adults in their lives. These programs are designed to bring together caring adults with children and youth. Mentoring programs can help ensure that young people have the guidance of adults who will take an interest in their well-being.

◈ Involve children and youth in activities with older adults (such as grandparents). For example, grandparents could be invited over for family meals. Grandparents could also take their grandchildren out—for example, to a movie, apple picking or to a local park or playground.

◈ Enrol young children—particularly children without siblings—in community programs or classes, or arrange play dates for them, so that they have opportunities to interact with other young children and find companionship outside the immediate family.

Parent relations

Healthy partnerships—that is, supportive, stable relationships, with an open display of love and warmth and good communication—between parents foster resilience in young people. Children imitate the love and affection they see between parents. While separation or divorce may break up partnerships and families, parents who no longer live together can still interact with one another and with their children in ways that encourage healthy development (for example, by speaking respectfully with one another, by making decisions jointly rather than giving two different messages about the same issue to the child, or by not putting the children in the middle of their own disputes).

Regardless of how happy a couple is, conflicts between partners are sometimes impossible to avoid. Children who grow up in homes filled with unresolved conflict are more likely to develop problems, such as aggressive behaviour, than those who grow up in peaceful homes. Resilient children are best able to detach themselves from family conflict.

The effects of conflicts will vary depending on the nature of the conflict, and how it's handled and solved. Some issues, such as deciding what to do for a family outing, are generally easier to work out. Other conflicts are more complicated. However, if parents can discuss their disagreements openly, can show their children how they can work out their problems and can agree on discipline and rules, their children are more likely to benefit.

Parents have their own risk factors, which can complicate their reactions to their children. Stress can be provoked by all kinds of situations. Some parents may be trying to manage with low incomes and poor housing, or may be in an unhappy relationship with their partner. Some parents may have been abused as children, so that having children triggers feelings from their own childhood. Newcomers to Canada may find that their skills and experience are not recognized here when they try to find work. Refugees may have posttraumatic stress after escaping violence in their home country.

RESILIENCE-BUILDING TIPS

The following strategies are intended specifically for parents

◈ Try couple therapy, if you have frequent arguments that you don't know how to solve by yourselves. Couple therapy can help partners find ways to manage issues in more positive ways; for instance, by meeting children's developmental needs rather than focusing on who is right or wrong. The children will benefit from a more peaceful household.

◈ Explore mediation therapy if you are separated or divorced, and the children are confused about their role in the family breakup. Mediation therapy that involves all family members can help parents understand and acknowledge that they remain parents for life despite any other disagreements they may have. This focuses parents' attention on meeting the needs of their children, rather than the children taking responsibility for the parents.

◈ Seek advice from an older and respected member of the family or community.

Parenting style

Effective parents are mindful, thoughtful and attuned to the particular needs and temperament of their children: they understand their children's developmental stages and corresponding physical, emotional and intellectual needs; and they recognize their strengths and limitations.

Parenting styles may be authoritarian, permissive, inconsistent or authoritative. The first three of these styles are the least favourable. Parents with an authoritarian style of parenting have rigid expectations around beliefs, behaviours and rules and give out harsh punishments when rules are broken. Parents with a permissive style set few rules and give their children little structure and guidance. And parents who are inconsistent (either together or individually) move between different parenting styles, so that their children never know what to expect.

Most researchers and parenting experts agree that an *authoritative* style *(see the following box for a definition)* is the ideal way to foster resilience in children. This style can be used by any adults who regularly interact with children, such as parents, daycare workers, teachers, school principals and coaches.

AUTHORITATIVE PARENTING

Parents who use an authoritative parenting style promote resilience in their children, because they:

- are warm, nurturing and loving, even when expressing disapproval of their children's behaviour

- provide firm, clearly defined rules and the reasons for the rules, while being flexible when they need to be

- let children know in advance what the consequences will be when rules are broken

- discipline constructively, fairly and consistently, recognizing that discipline is a form of teaching, not punishment

- apologize to their children when they are wrong

- have appropriate expectations of their children, which are in keeping with their children's physical, emotional and intellectual stages of development
- praise their children for their efforts and accomplishments
- comfort their children when they're upset
- take part in their children's activities
- teach decision-making and problem-solving skills (*see page 45*)
- teach social skills, including the value of patience, co-operation, empathy, forgiveness and apologies
- monitor their children's friends and activities to ensure that their children are safe and that the activities are appropriate to their age and developmental stage
- use reasoning and persuasion, instead of verbal or physical abuse
- discuss issues and listen respectfully
- admire, respect, like and trust their children
- allow their children to experience difficulties and help them find solutions without being overprotective
- show their children how to learn from mistakes
- involve children in decisions that affect them and celebrate their wise choices
- encourage adolescents to develop their own opinions and beliefs
- accept and respect their teens' increasing need for independence
- speak optimistically about the future.

WHAT EFFECT DOES AN AUTHORITATIVE PARENTING STYLE HAVE ON CHILDREN AND YOUTH?

Research has shown that young people raised by authoritative parents:

- are psychologically healthier than those raised by parents with other parenting styles

- are more open to their parents' guidance and, as a result, have better social skills

- develop the skills to control their anger

- are confident and develop a sense of responsibility

- develop the ability to reason

- have problem-solving and decision-making skills

- understand the consequences of their actions

- are resilient.

RESILIENCE-BUILDING TIPS

The following strategies are intended specifically for parents

◈ Learn an authoritative style to working with your children by enrolling in Parent Management Skills Training (PMST) programs, offered by many social service agencies, to improve your child-rearing methods. These programs show how to set clear and consistent rules, and how to discipline children appropriately in ways that teach rather than punish.

◈ Help your children understand what you expect of them. Expectations prevent children from becoming confused and anxious. When they know what to expect, they don't have to guess and this reduces their frustration.

Sibling relations

Healthy relationships between brothers and sisters, or siblings, develop when families encourage sharing and co-operation, and discourage competition. Families with one child can also encourage these positive behaviours by giving their child chances to share and co-operate with cousins and friends. Many other factors also contribute to the quality of sibling relations. These factors include the children's age and birth order, the number of brothers and sisters in a family, the parents' style of parenting, and the presence of new siblings as a result of birth, adoption or blended families.

The physical or mental health of siblings can also affect the sibling relationship. For example, in some families, if one child has a problem (for example, aggression or substance use) that requires a lot of the parents' time and attention, the other siblings can feel left out and ignored. In other families, however, the challenge of living with or helping a sibling with a problem can build resilience in the other siblings, as they develop strategies to cope with their sibling's disability. Regardless of their situation, young people want to feel as important, wanted and needed as their brothers and sisters.

RESILIENCE-BUILDING TIPS

◈ Dedicate some special time for each child. If the family situation is stressful, spend time doing an activity the child enjoys outside the home.

◈ Involve youth in Boy Scouts, Girl Guides and youth-assisting-youth organizations to give them a healthy growing environment and special time for themselves.

◈ Encourage co-operation instead of competition among siblings.

◈ Recognize and work with each child's unique strengths and challenges. For instance, if a boy has a musical talent, involve him in a music class, or if a girl is athletic, register her in a sports league.

Parents' health

Parents who experience good physical and mental health are more likely to be able to respond well to their children's needs and to develop a caring relationship with them. Parents who take the time to look after themselves (as well as their children) contribute to the well-being and resilience of their children. Of course, taking good care of themselves can be a challenge for many parents who have money or job problems, a sick child or relative to look after, the challenge of juggling care of multiple children and other competing demands for their time, or their own health problems.

An added challenge is created by the trend toward having children later in life: parents are more likely to be coping with—rather than getting support from—their own aging parents, while potentially having more health issues themselves. On the other hand, an advantage with older parents is that they may be more mature, have greater stability in their relationship with their partner and have more financial stability.

Parents with a serious, chronic physical or mental health problem often have a hard time meeting their children's psychological needs for attention and nurturing, particularly if much of their time is focused around their own illness. As a result, family life can be chaotic and unpredictable, with the potential for the children to be neglected, or for children to take on a parenting role, if the caregiving parent is too physically or emotionally exhausted. Parents who are depressed, for example, are more likely to be tired and withdrawn and to feel hopeless or pessimistic about the future.

How children respond to a parent's health problem will depend on several factors, including their own resilience, their parent's behaviour, their understanding of their parent's problem and how well other family members are able to cope. Having a parent with a mental health or physical problem does not always negatively affect the child. The child may manage fine, if, for instance, the well parent can be supportive, the child realizes he or she is not to blame for the problem, and the parent's behaviour is not changed dramatically by the health problem. If the parent's problem is very serious, and has lasted a long time, putting stress on all the family members, then the child is more likely to be affected. Parents could discuss the parent's health problems with their children, so that the children can understand what the parent is dealing with and how they can better live with the problem. There are many books, available through parenting bookstores, that help to explain mental or physical health problems to a child. *(Two examples, both published by CAMH, are listed in "Resources" on page 95.)*

Children are more likely to be resilient, despite living with a parent with, for example, a mental health or substance use problem, if they have another parent who is healthy. Some children will, in fact, become more self-confident and develop greater problem-solving skills by helping the parent with a problem. This is more likely to occur if the children understand that they are not responsible for their parent's difficulties, and if the parent does not behave in a way that is directly harmful to them.

RESILIENCE-BUILDING TIPS

If a parent has a health problem

◈ Find other adults (such as grandparents, an aunt or a friend) or hire a nanny or babysitter to spend time with the children.

◈ Eat healthy food, exercise, get plenty of sleep (if possible) and take the time to do hobbies and activities that give you pleasure and relieve stress.

◈ Get appropriate medical care and follow recommended treatment plans to reduce the impact of the mental health problem on your children.

Support outside the family

Supportive family networks and other resources are essential for young people's healthy development. In instances where parents are physically or emotionally absent or struggling with other problems, adults who are not part of the immediate family (such as a family friend, teacher or parent of a child's friend) can become active in the child's life, establishing much-needed care, guidance and support. A strong bond with just one adult has been shown to boost young people's ability to be resilient. Young people need adults' time and involvement in their lives; they also need practical advice and emotional support.

Outside support is particularly crucial for new mothers, who have a 13 per cent risk of developing postpartum depression following the birth of a child. Because caring for an infant can be isolating, and new parents benefit from the feedback and companionship of other parents, being connected to different community programs and parenting groups can be helpful.

RESILIENCE-BUILDING TIPS

◆ Encourage youth to get involved in recreation programs offered through community centres or after-school programs where they can connect with other supportive adults or find friends their own age whom they can confide in.

◆ Encourage young people to speak to a teacher or school counsellor they trust and feel comfortable talking to.

◆ Turn to health and social service agencies for support. They will decide if counselling is needed or whether parents would benefit from practical help with housing, welfare or other social services.

◆ Help new parents to connect to parenting programs offered through public health, parenting centres and community centres, such as mother and toddler programs or play groups.

Summary

Family factors affecting the resilience of children and youth

PROTECTIVE FACTORS	RISK FACTORS
○ secure attachment to a parent or caregiver	○ lack of caring parent or other adult
○ a caring, supportive adult outside the family or supportive extended family	○ overly controlling parents
	○ living with a parent who has a substance use or mental health problem
○ warmth and affection	○ little parental supervision
○ open communication	○ lack of structure and regular routines
○ living with two nurturing parents	○ living with family problems (for example, violence in the home, conflicts between parents or siblings)
○ parents with an authoritative parenting style, establishing clear, reasonable and consistent rules and expectations	○ harsh discipline or punishment
○ appropriate supervision	○ loss of a parent at an early age
○ family who spend time together and collectively participate and contribute to family life	○ absent parents (for example, due to parent being in hospital or jail)
○ ability to resolve conflicts as a family	○ lack of consistency (for example, due to parent's problems with alcohol or other drugs)
○ presence of family rituals (for example, celebrating birthdays)	○ parents' hostile separation or divorce
	○ child abuse or neglect
	○ low family income

5

Enhancing resilience:
Environmental factors

PERSONAL STORY OF RESILIENCE

James Bartleman was born in 1939 in Orillia, Ontario, to a Scottish-Canadian father and an Aboriginal mother. Though in his early years he felt the love and warmth of his family, he also faced poverty and discrimination as a member of the First Nations community. As a youth, he thought he would spend the rest of his life as a low-income labourer.

But Bartleman's life turned around: he discovered the village library, became an avid reader and did well in school. When a generous American offered to send him off to finish high school in a distant community and then to university, he was able to take full advantage of the opportunity.

In 1963 Bartleman earned an Honours BA in history from the University of Western Ontario. The degree launched a distinguished career spanning more than 35 years in the Canadian Foreign Service. Bartleman has served as Canada's ambassador to Cuba, Israel, NATO and the European Union and as high commissioner to Cyprus, South Africa and Australia. He was the foreign and defence policy adviser to the prime minister of Canada. And he has written best-selling books: Out of Muskoka, On Six Continents, Rollercoaster *and* Raisin Wine.

In 2002, he was sworn in as the 27th lieutenant-governor of Ontario. In 2004, as part of his mandate to encourage literacy in Aboriginal young people, he launched an official book program that provided 850,000 gently used books to set up libraries in First Nations schools and Native friendship centres. He has also established literacy summer camps in 28 northern First Nations communities and launched "Club Amick," a young readers' program, whereby 3,500 youth in the far north receive a club newsletter and a new book several times a year.

Despite an extraordinary career, Bartleman has had to cope with depression. Throughout his term in office as the Queen's representative, he has spoken out against the stigma (prejudice and discrimination) associated with mental health problems. In 2004, he received a Courage to Come Back Award from the Centre for Addiction and Mental Health for his resilience and recovery and for giving back to the community by talking about his experience and helping others. ☙

5

As is true of all people who are resilient, James Bartleman's resilience was due to an interplay of factors. Bartleman realized at an early age that literacy and a good education were the keys to self-fulfilment and success. He also appreciated that the hardships he underwent early in his life were learning experiences, giving him insights that, among other things, have allowed him to champion the cause of mental health. His experience with depression demonstrates how people who are resilient can still have mental health problems.

Social determinants of resilience

A growing body of research indicates that our health and well-being is affected not only by individual attributes and choices but also—and at times more importantly—by socio-economic conditions. In this book we apply the concept of social determinants of health to resilience (*for a full discussion of various dimensions of the social determinants of health, see Public Health Agency of Canada under "References"*). By doing so, we recognize that children's and youth's resilience develops out of a combination of their individual, family and environmental factors. In this chapter we focus on environmental factors.

The characteristics of the environments (communities or societies) in which people live can profoundly affect their health, growth and resilience. Environmental factors occur at many levels, including local (neighbourhood), national (Canada) and global (other places in the world). Environmental factors affecting the resilience of young people include physical conditions (for example, young people's access to good food, housing, schools, parks, resources and recreational activities) and those related to social conditions (for example, income disparities; employment equity; and young people's inclusion and sense of belonging in communities and society at large regardless of their gender, ethnicity, ability or sexual orientation). While recognizing the importance of physical conditions on the healthy development of children and youth, the focus in this book is on social conditions. Social conditions interact with young people's individual factors (such as their thoughts about, experience of and reactions to their social conditions) and affect how resilient they will be.

Promoting mental health and resilience at an environmental level means having in place practices, policies and laws that bring about fairness of opportunities (such as universal access to education, health and social services); social justice (such as eliminating prejudice and discrimination); and mutual respect for everyone's gender, culture, sexual orientation, religion and spirituality, neighbourhood, job, financial situation and abilities.

Key environmental factors affecting resilience

The environmental factors we address in this chapter are organized into four main areas affecting the resilience of children and youth. This is a new way of looking at mental health—the factors we discuss have often not been recognized as directly affecting resilience when, in fact, they affect it a great deal.

- Inclusion: Having a sense of belonging
  - gender
  - culture

- Social conditions: Society promoting resilience
  - socio-economic situation
  - media influences

- Access: Systems promoting resilience

  - education

  - health

- Involvement: Youth participation in the world around them

Inclusion: Having a sense of belonging

We've talked about the resilience of young people and the resilience of families. Communities also vary in terms of their own resilience, and in how they promote young people's resilience.

Social communities can be local, national or international. They form around the shared characteristics of members, such as age, sexual orientation, the school they attend, abilities, interests, religion and spirituality, gender and culture. We are part of many social communities at one time: for instance, we are a certain age, we may be affiliated with a religious or spiritual group and come from a certain culture. We may identify with and see ourselves as belonging to a community, or society may identify us as being part of the community.

Inclusive social communities are those that embrace and accept everyone and create opportunities for each person to reach his or her potential. Inclusive social communities bring about true belonging through social and economic justice; equity and fairness; and acceptance of and respect for diversity. Inclusion involves removing barriers and providing supports.

Inclusion is linked to positive health outcomes while exclusion is linked to poor health outcomes. To be resilient and have good mental health, young people need to feel included and respected in their community. Each young person is an individual with unique characteristics. Young people accept and value themselves when they are included and valued by others. Yet some young people feel they don't fit into various communities because of their differences. Young people who are newcomers or First Nations, for example, may feel they don't belong to Canadian culture or their school culture because of language and other barriers. They may feel they are looked down upon, feared or even ignored because of their differences. They may face racism, isolation and poverty. And, because of these difficulties, they may feel vulnerable, do poorly at school or have few friends. If, however, these young people are accepted and included by others, they are more likely to embrace and celebrate their differences despite the challenges they face. Being accepted contributes to positive self-esteem and increased resilience. It is easier to feel good about ourselves when we live in an environment that permits and encourages a diversity of values and is accepting of a wide range of self-expression.

There are many ways young people can identify themselves. In working with children and youth, it is important to understand which identities are most meaningful for them. Often people identify with a combination of characteristics (for example, age group and youth trends). Here we focus on gender and culture, because they are two particularly strong aspects of how we identify ourselves.

GENDER

Among the most important ways people identify themselves is as male, female or having various attributes of each. Biology accounts for differences in boys' and girls' physical characteristics. However, not so obvious are the attitudes, behaviours and values about gender laid out by society and reinforced by parents, peers, communities and the media. Encouraging young people to recognize and evaluate assigned gender roles and stereotypes helps them develop a positive sense of themselves. For example, we can encourage girls who like mathematics and boys who want to be nurses to pursue their career goals. Young people who ignore gender-role stereotypes can serve as examples for future generations.

RESILIENCE-BUILDING TIPS

◈ Teach children and youth to have a positive attitude about both genders.

◈ Help young people recognize that gender roles are not inborn. Gender roles are socially constructed—they can vary from culture to culture as well as over time.

◈ Promote and support gender equality across systems (for example, in schools and in workplaces).

CULTURE

Having a strong cultural identity is another important part of young people's self-concept. As with gender, society's acceptance or judgment of young people's culture can affect their resilience. Societies that are accepting of all cultures and diversity promote positive cultural identities in young people. Having a sense of belonging is important for our mental health.

As a result of changing migration trends, Canada's cultural diversity is increasing, especially in cities. Some young people are newcomers to Canada; some have parents or grandparents who are newcomers; and some have Canadian roots that extend back for generations. Many young people live in families that have practices and values different from Canada's Aboriginal, English and French populations—and their families often differ in terms of how much they have integrated or assimilated into Canadian culture.

Young people may live within two (or perhaps more) cultures—their original culture and Canadian culture—and continually move back and forth between them. Those who are able to feel comfortable in both cultures and move freely between them have a greater sense of belonging, and are more resilient.

It's not unusual for young people to question their self-worth when they find themselves in a new environment where they cannot speak the language well and where the customs and belief systems differ from those they experience at home. They may get low marks in school and have few friends—not due to a lack of intelligence or social skills, but simply because they cannot communicate well in the new language. All these factors can affect their resilience.

As parents, teachers and community members, we can be role models for young people. We can help them feel good about their cultural identity (or any other identities they may have) and can help them deal with prejudice and discrimination. Even better, we can work to create a society that welcomes diversity. Creating this kind of society can play a key role in children and youth feeling free to express and be proud of their unique identities and diversities.

An inclusive society helps young people to feel like they belong and can take part in civic responsibilities as members of society. Making young people feel included is a key part of building resilience.

RESILIENCE-BUILDING TIPS

◆ Show sensitivity and respect for all cultures and traditions—and teach young people to do the same.

◆ Connect young people to culturally appropriate services if they are available.

◆ Educate yourselves about the various groups to which Canadian young people belong, particularly when you are working with children and youth from a background you are unfamiliar with.

◆ Find opportunities for youth to meet, discuss values, take leadership roles and explore their responsibilities to society.

◆ Accept young people for who they are and work to eliminate negative stereotypes, prejudice and discrimination.

Social conditions: Society promoting resilience

Young people's *social conditions* are influenced by their family's level of education and income; the kinds of neighbourhoods they live in; access to services (for example, recreation, health, transportation, police); whether or not they experience racism, sexism or other forms of prejudice and discrimination; and the kinds of images they see of young people like themselves on TV, in movies and in magazines. Young people's social identities are influenced by their gender, sexual orientation, religion or spirituality, culture, languages spoken and nationality.

In this section, we focus on two important social influences on young people: their socio-economic situation and the media. We recognize that many other influences can affect children and youth's resilience as well, but their socio-economic situation and the media are two particularly powerful influences—socio-economic situation because it affects many aspects of our lives; and the media because it affects young people's attitudes and behaviours and how they are viewed by the rest of society.

SOCIO-ECONOMIC SITUATION

Adults' income, job and education level determine their social and economic situation, and that of their family. Until young people are old enough to support themselves, they must rely on their parents to provide them with nutritious food, safe housing, adequate clothing and access to good schools and recreational activities. Meeting these basic needs provides young people with a solid foundation to build resilience.

However, parents don't always have the power to provide their children with these basic needs. Families with low incomes may have difficulty feeding their children healthy food and finding decent housing. Some may be forced to live in neighbour-hoods with a lot of noise, crime, pollution and inadequate social services—in part because this is the only kind of neighbourhood they can afford. Still others may not be able to find a job because their work experience from another country is not recognized in Canada.

It takes time, will and long-term commitment to create the kind of society in which necessary supports and services are funded and in place. All young people benefit from having the right supports in place: they face fewer barriers and have a greater chance of reaching their potential and of being resilient.

RESILIENCE-BUILDING TIPS

❖ Work to persuade neighbourhood, municipal, provincial and federal governments and associations to adequately fund programs that will help support young people and their families, with the aim of providing:
- safe, affordable housing, schools and communities
- nutritional programs in schools and in the community
- adequate child care
- high-quality public schools
- skills training and job-creation programs for adults
- adequate wages, employee benefits (such as time off work to raise children) and employment insurance benefits
- recognition of educational and professional qualifications obtained in other countries

- free (or reduced fee) English as a Second Language (ESL) training
- free (or reduced fee) access to neighbourhood activities, such as sports, art, music, dance and gymnastics
- a one-stop resource centre to help people find needed services.

◈ Work to achieve the above-mentioned goals by, for example:
  - forming and participating in neighbourhood, school and other committees to make social changes and help each other out in times of need
  - putting pressure on governments—through telephone calls, letters and petitions.

MEDIA MESSAGES

Media compete with parents and other important people in children's and youth's lives in passing on learning, ideas, views, beliefs, culture, traditions and values. Most Canadian young people receive daily messages and images through various forms of media, such as television, newspapers, magazines, books, music, films, video games and the Internet.

Media messages can help or harm young people. For example, teenagers may watch the news on TV and hear messages and see images that present unrealistic or too-narrow ideas of what is an average and normal youth. Or the ideas being presented may conflict with what their families have told them and make them confused. Media messages and images can have their most profound effects on adolescents who are experimenting with new behaviours and trying on new identities as they figure out who they are and who they want to be.

Media can be particularly harmful to the self-esteem of young girls (and, increasingly, young boys). As adults, we need to talk with girls about having a healthy, realistic body image. We can inform them that the images of women that they see on television and in magazines do not represent the norm and may be enhanced by makeup, lighting techniques and computers. We need to remind girls (and, increasingly, boys as well) that the way they look is only one—and not the most important—aspect of what makes them who they are.

We also need to teach young people to be aware and cautious of the media, while also exposing them to healthy alternatives to its influences (such as playing sports and doing volunteer work). However, we must recognize that the media can play a positive role in their lives as well. Cable and specialty channels allow young people to watch a wide range of educational programs in fields such as history, geography and science. The Internet enables them to quickly access information on an almost unlimited number of topics. Young people today live in an interconnected global village.

RESILIENCE-BUILDING TIPS

◈ Lobby governments to develop and maintain guidelines for programming directed at children and youth.

◈ Support media that:
  - portray young people engaging in leadership roles and healthy activities
  - involve children and youth, allowing them to publish or broadcast their views
  - sponsor youth sports and activities
  - provide coverage of young people's local and national events
  - encourage creativity
  - restrict portrayals of violence.

◈ Help young people to challenge or think critically about media messages and images, especially those that glamourize violence, smoking and other substance use, and unhealthy sexual behaviours; that portray unrealistic body shapes; or that stereotype or discriminate against people.

◈ Put pressure on the media to accurately and realistically portray young people with diverse looks and levels of ability.

Access: Systems promoting resilience

Young people access and are affected by many systems in society, particularly the education and health systems (including public health). Some young people and their families—especially those with special needs—may also access the social service system, such as agencies offering or advocating for child welfare and income support services.

EDUCATION

Children and adolescents spend a significant part of their time at school.

Curriculum standards for schools ensure students receive knowledge and skills appropriate for their age and grade level, with the goal of preparing them for the world they will enter once they leave school. But schools can, and most often do, offer more than academic training. When successful, they also give children and youth opportunities to develop socially and emotionally.

The sooner in a child's life that we begin to promote protective factors for resilience, the greater the chance that these factors will have a positive effect. For instance, research shows that universal, publicly funded early childhood education and care programs help to build resilience in young people. These programs—which include government-regulated centres, home daycares, junior kindergarten programs, nursery schools and preschools—enable parents to work outside of the home or pursue their own education. If they are of high quality, these programs provide the kind of intellectual and social stimulation that promote the mental development and social abilities of children—qualities that provide the basis for their later success at school and the foundation for a healthy adult life.

Canada is an increasingly diverse nation—and young people arrive at school with varied life experiences and skills. Schools that respond to and respect students from all backgrounds, and with varying levels of readiness for school, increase the likelihood that each student will reach his or her potential.

RESILIENCE-BUILDING TIPS

Schools can

◈ Provide opportunities for students to take on responsibility, problem-solve and make decisions (for example, by publishing a school newspaper).

◈ Offer programs that involve young people in volunteer community work, such as helping out at seniors' centres and hospitals.

◈ Set effective policies and procedures to prevent harassment, bullying and other forms of violence.

◈ Provide daily physical activity.

◈ Have English-as-a-Second-Language (ESL) programs for newcomer students.

◈ Provide mental health services and special education for students who are having difficulty academically or socially.

◈ Offer programs that help mentally and physically challenged students take part in school life.

◈ Encourage acceptance and respect for all students through programs and policies that encourage attitudes and behaviours free of sexism, racism, homophobia and other forms of prejudice and discrimination.

◈ Offer free or low-cost programs for parents to learn skills (such as parent-training programs) and relieve stress (such as yoga classes).

◈ Provide adequate supports (for example, note-takers, recording equipment, Braille computers) for students with disabilities.

◈ Employ class assistants, guidance counsellors and school nurses.

◈ Hire staff that represent the varied backgrounds of the students attending the school.

Parents and teachers can

◈ Get involved in their child's education by, for example, participating on boards, in the classroom and in fundraising initiatives.

◈ Help develop an orientation program to welcome students— paying special attention to students who are new to the school (starting elementary, middle or secondary school; or arriving from another school district or from another country).

◈ Lobby governments and workplaces to provide bursaries and scholarships that encourage young people to get post-secondary training and education: this type of financial support should be able to benefit young people living in remote areas, as well as those with disabilities.

◈ Promote a variety of career paths for boys and girls, including non-traditional careers (such as engineering for young women and nursing for young men).

HEALTH

The health system includes people and agencies involved with health promotion, prevention and treatment. Young people and their families use the health system from the moment they're born and continue to use its many services throughout their lives. To promote the well-being of people, we also need healthy and safe environments and policies that support these environments.

The social determinants of health have a powerful effect on the health and well-being of the population. Young people's resilience is best supported when social and economic conditions—along with family and community resources and support— work together for young people's optimal growth and development. We need funding support from various levels of government to enhance the public health system and champion programs and policies that endorse taking a broad approach to promoting the well-being of children and youth and their families.

The health system, along with education and social services, plays an important role through different phases of young people's growth and development. These systems can work together to provide appropriate services and support for young people and their immediate family members, while striving for minimal disruption to their education.

RESILIENCE-BUILDING TIPS

Pressure governments to

◈ Provide expectant mothers with free and easy access to good health care (including prenatal care classes that emphasize healthy practices while pregnant).

◈ Offer supports for new mothers around breastfeeding and infant care.

◈ Launch information campaigns on healthy lifestyle choices targeted at children and young teens.

◈ Support research and pass legislation to restrict or ban the use of environmental contaminants (such as pesticides) that can harm pregnant women, developing fetuses and young children.

◈ Support public health campaigns to inform parents how cigarette smoking and exposure to second-hand smoke can harm fetuses and young people and pressure them to enact by-laws to make public places smoke-free.

◈ Provide supports for children whose parents have addiction and mental health problems.

◈ Provide age- and gender-specific programs for youth.

◈ Provide culturally appropriate counselling and health care for youth.

Involvement: Youth's participation in the world around them

Meaningful participation in activities in the home, school and community contributes to the resilience of children and youth. At home, parents can give young people chores that are appropriate for their age and skills. In this way, children contribute to the home's upkeep while learning important life skills and developing a sense of responsibility. At school, young people can take part in clubs and extracurricular activities: parents and teachers can encourage them to get involved in student government bodies and school planning committees (such as bullying prevention committees). In the broader community, young people can get involved in neighbourhood and civic events that instil in them a sense of responsibility and duty to others locally and globally.

Participating in physical activities (such as informal play, organized sports or individual activities) does more than build healthy bodies. Physical activities can provide opportunities for emotional growth as young people adjust to, respond to and cope with new challenges. They can help young people relieve stress. And they can teach young people what it means to be a "good sport"—such as learning how to take their turn; how to follow rules; how to work co-operatively toward a common goal; how to learn from facing the disappointment of a loss; and how to learn from the loss to then improve their skills. Being a good sport also involves having the grace to congratulate the winner for a game well played and not teasing or taunting the person or team that didn't win.

Young people can also benefit from individual, non-competitive sports, such as skiing, swimming or skating. They can learn, for example, how to set goals for themselves and face their fears.

Through non-physical recreational activities, such as playing chess or learning to play an instrument, children and youth develop social and other skills in supportive environments that challenge them to excel. They develop friendships outside the family with peers and caring adults, such as coaches and music teachers.

Being involved in school and other activities is particularly helpful for young people who have challenging home lives, such as having to cope with an abusive or unwell parent. Activities that they find enjoyable can help distract young people from problems at home. Through a cultural or debating club, for example, young people can find comfort among like-minded peers, a sense of belonging and accomplishment, and perhaps a connection with another caring adult who acts as a role model and provides support.

Resilience is further enhanced in young people who get involved in community and volunteer work. Some school boards offer students the opportunity to participate in community service activities to gain a high school credit. By doing volunteer work, young people can then apply what they've learned at home and at school in real-life situations that help other people. Benefits include opportunities to work co-operatively with others, practise decision-making and problem-solving skills, develop empathy and enhance social skills.

Participating in household, school and community activities helps reduce the risk of engaging in negative behaviours, such as aggression. It also increases young people's sense of connection and their capacity for resilience, while decreasing their sense of isolation.

RESILIENCE-BUILDING TIPS

❖ Involve youth in decision-making forums of organizations and social systems that they use and are a part of. Youth need to know that they have a say in their lives, and that what they say matters.

❖ Encourage young people to participate in volunteer and other community activities, and instil in them a sense of responsibility to do so.

❖ Lobby workplaces to help young people learn by setting up joint programs with schools and other organizations, by offering career-day events, as well as by providing young people with meaningful work opportunities through co-operative and apprenticeship programs. Workplaces could, for example, donate used computers and other multimedia equipment to schools and youth-serving organizations; sponsor events such as science fairs; and support young people's sports teams.

Summary

Environmental factors affecting the resilience of children and youth

PROTECTIVE FACTORS	RISK FACTORS
O policies at local, provincial and national levels that promote equity, justice and inclusion	O experiencing racism, sexism, homophobia or other forms of prejudice and discrimination
O an equal chance to fulfil goals without facing prejudice or discrimination	O marginalization or isolation produced by inequitable opportunities
O access to social support networks	
O access to community resources, such as public transportation	O living in a family with economic difficulties
O caring, supportive and safe school environments	O living in an unsafe neighbourhood
O involvement in healthy day-to-day physical and recreational activities	O living in a neighbourhood without adequate public services and social supports
O doing volunteer activities	
O access to counsellors and mental health and addiction services when needed	O frequently changing schools and neighbour-hoods
O living in a safe neighbourhood free of crime and violence	O language barriers
O living in a caring neighbourhood or community	
O positive media messages	
O contact with other caring adults and role models, such as teachers, coaches, spiritual leaders and neighbours	
O links to a strong cultural community, giving young people a sense of history, feelings of belonging, and self-esteem	
O opportunities for problem solving and decision making at various levels	

Glossary

References

Resources

Glossary

adolescence: the period between childhood and adulthood when youth mature physically and emotionally

aggression: an action or threat of action that is intended to harm another person, either physically or psychologically

attachment: the relationship of trust that forms between infants and parents: when securely attached, infants feel confident that the people looking after them will satisfy their needs and keep them safe

children: boys or girls from birth to age 12

cognitive-behavioural therapy: a type of psychotherapy in which people learn to look at how their beliefs or thoughts affect the way that they look at themselves and the world

community: a group of people sharing a common bond

cultural identity: how people see themselves in different roles and relationships that are related to their feelings of belonging to a particular culture *(see definition of* culture*)*

culture: all of a society's patterns of behaviour, music, art, dance, writings, crafts, foods, architecture, beliefs and all other products of its human work and thought, considered together as a whole

discipline: training used by parents to help their children learn to behave in ways that are acceptable and agreeable to others

discrimination: the negative and unfair treatment of a person or a group of people due to prejudiced views *(see definition of prejudice)*

economic: relating to the wealth (for example, money, resources, possessions) of people, communities and nations

empathy: the ability to understand and relate to the feelings, situations and motives of others

environment: the whole physical, natural, social and cultural world in which a person lives

family therapy: a form of psychotherapy (sometimes called "talk therapy") used to help family members increase their understanding of each other and improve their communication

gender: females or males considered as a category or group that is not necessarily defined by physical or biological factors

gender role: a pattern of human behaviour that is considered by a particular culture to be either male or female

homophobia: irrational fear, hatred, prejudice or negative attitudes toward homosexuality and people who are gay, lesbian or bisexual

identity: how people see themselves in different roles and relationships

media: methods of mass communication, such as newspapers, magazines, radio, CDs, television, movies, DVDs and the Internet

mental health: a feeling of well-being in which people are able to use their abilities to think, feel, act and interact—in order to function at home, at school, at work and in other places and situations, and to generally take part in everyday life and enjoy themselves

mental health problems: problems that affect people's abilities to think and feel and that prevent them from taking part in everyday life

mental health promotion: strategies, programs and policies directed at all levels of society (from individual to community to national) with the purpose of promoting the mental well-being of all people

mentoring programs: programs, such as those run by the international Big Brothers Big Sisters organization, designed to bring together caring adults with children and youth: the adults act as positive role models, providing friendship, advising and helping young people to reach their potential

newcomer: a person who has recently arrived in a country, either as a visitor, resident, immigrant or refugee

nuclear family: a family made up of a mother and father and their children

optimistic: holding a positive view of the future

parents: biological, adoptive or foster parents; guardians; primary caregivers; and any people who are primarily responsible for the raising of a child

pessimistic: holding a negative view of the future

prejudice: a negative view of a person or group of people, formed without reasonable knowledge and sometimes involving suspicion or hatred of the person or group

protective factors: characteristics of individuals, their families and their communities or environments that increase the likelihood of resilience

racism: the false view that race can determine differences in people's characters or abilities or that a particular race is better than others

risk factors: characteristics of individuals, their families and their communities or environments that decrease the likelihood of resilience

self-concept: how we view and understand ourselves

self-esteem: how we judge our self-worth and understand ourselves in comparison to others

sexism: the false view that a person's sex can determine his or her character or ability or that one sex is better than another

sexual orientation: the direction of an individual's sexual interest toward either members of the same, opposite or both sexes

social: anything involving relationships between humans

social skills: the ways and abilities that people use in interacting and co-operating with others

society: all of the relationships between humans living in a group considered together as a single whole

socio-economic: related to the interaction of social and economic factors

stereotype: an overly simple label or preconceived idea about a group

stigma: negative attitudes (prejudice) and negative behaviour (discrimination) toward people with substance use and mental health problems

temperament: inborn and acquired characteristics that influence how people relate to others around them, and how they respond to situations they are presented with

therapy: a supportive interaction between a person and a therapist around mental health or substance use problems. The therapist helps to clarify, support, explore and encourage the person who is having difficulties, so that he or she can build better ways of coping, increase self-esteem and grow personally.

young people: children and youth from birth to age 19

youth: boys or girls aged 13 to 19

References

Alberta Alcohol and Drug Abuse Commission. (2003, May). *Youth Risk and Protective Factors*. Edmonton: Author. Available: www.aadac.com. Accessed on May 3, 2007.

Alperstein, G. & Raman, S. (2003). Promoting mental health and emotional well-being among children and youth: A role for community child health? *Child: Care, Health & Development, 29* (4), 269–274.

American Psychological Association. (2002). *Developing Adolescents: A Reference for Professionals*. Washington: Author.

Barankin, T. & Greenberg, M. (1996). The impact of parental affective disorders on families. In B. Abosh & A. Collins (Eds.), *Mental Illness in the Family: Issues and Trends.* (pp. 105–119). Toronto: University of Toronto Press.

Barankin, T., Konstantareas, M. & deBosset, F. (1989, August). Adaptation of Soviet Jewish immigrants and their children to Toronto. *Canadian Journal of Psychiatry, 34,* 512–518.

Beardslee, W.R. & Podorefsky, D. (1988). Resilient adolescents whose parents have serious affective and other psychiatric disorders. *American Journal of Psychiatry, 145* (1), 63–69.

Benard, B. (2004). *Resiliency: What We Have Learned*. San Francisco: WestEd.

Branden, N. (1995). *Six Pillars of Self-Esteem*. New York: Bantam Books.

Browne, G. & Friendly, M. (2002). *Early Childhood Education and Care as a Determinant of Health*. Ottawa: Health Canada. Available: www.phac-aspc.gc.ca/ph-sp/phdd/overview_implications/07_ecec.html. Accessed on November 13, 2006.

Canadian Council on Social Development. (2006). *The Progress of Canada's Children and Youth 2006*. Available: www.ccsd.ca/pccy/2006. Accessed on November 13, 2006.

Cauchon, C. (1994). Whistler's mutter: Self-talk. *Psychology Today*. Available: http://cms.psychologytoday.com/articles/pto-19940901-000016.html. Accessed on November 13, 2006.

Centre for Addiction and Mental Health. (2003). *Challenges & Choices: Finding Mental Health Services in Ontario*. Toronto: Author.

Centre for Addiction and Mental Health Foundation. (2004). 2004 Courage to Come Back Awards. *Spring 2004 Newsletter.* Available: www.camh.net/Foundation/Publications/Foundation_Progress_Reports/ Newsletter_Spring_2004/courage_insert_sum04.pdf. Accessed on November 13, 2006.

Centre for Health Promotion. (1997). *Proceedings from the International Workshop on Mental Health Promotion.* Toronto: University of Toronto.

Chess, S. & Thomas, A. (1986). *Temperament in Clinical Practice.* New York: Guilford Press.

Children of Alcoholics Foundation. (1992). *Report of the Forum on Protective Factors, Resiliency, and Vulnerable Children.* New York: Author.

Cloitre, M., Morin, N.A. & Linares, L.O. (2004, January/February). Children's resilience in the face of trauma. *Child Study Center Letter, 8* (3), 1–6.

Crust, L. (No Date). Sport psychology—Thought control. *Peak Performance.* Available: www.pponline.co.uk/aboutus.html. Accessed on November 13, 2006.

Fay, M. (April 2004). Count me in! *Ontario Health Promotion E-Mail Bulletin #358,* 1.

Galabuzi, G. & Labonte, R. (2002). *Social Inclusion as a Determinant of Health.* Ottawa: Health Canada.

Gibbs, J. (2001). *Tribes: A New Way of Being and Learning Together.* Santa Rosa, CA: Center Source Systems.

Gorman, D., Brough, M. & Ramirez, E. (2003). How young people from culturally and linguistically diverse backgrounds experience mental health: Some insights for mental health nurses. *International Journal of Mental Health Nursing, 12,* 194–202.

Health Canada. (1999). *Healthy Development of Children and Youth: The Role of the Determinants of Health.* Ottawa: Author.

Health Canada. (2001, April). *Mental Health Promotion: Promoting Mental Health Means Promoting the Best of Ourselves FAQs (Frequently Asked Questions).* Ottawa: Author.

Health Canada. (2002). Infant attachment: Helpful things for parents/caregivers to know. *First Connections . . . make all the difference.* Available: www.phac-aspc.gc.ca/mh-sm/mhp-psm/pub/ fc-pc/par_needtoknow.html. Accessed on November 22, 2006.

Henderson, N. (2003a). Hard-wired to bounce back. *The Prevention Researcher, 10,* 5–7.

Henderson, N. (2003b). The resiliency route to academic success. *Partnerships: A Guide for Counselors and Teachers, No. 113.* Philadelphia: Laboratory for Student Success.

Joubert, J. & Raeburn, J. (1998). Mental health promotion: People, power and passion. *International Journal of Mental Health Promotion,* September, 15–22.

Katz, L. (1995, Summer). *How Can We Strengthen Children's Self-Esteem?* Urbana, IL: ERIC Clearinghouse on Elementary and Early Childhood Education.

Khanlou, N. (2003). Mental health promotion education in multicultural settings. *Nurse Education Today, 23,* 96–103.

Khanlou, N. (2004). Influences on adolescent self-esteem in multicultural Canadian secondary schools. *Public Health Nursing, 21* (5), 404–411.

Khanlou, N. (2005). Cultural identity as part of youth's self-concept in multicultural settings. *eCommunity: International Journal of Mental Health & Addiction, 3* (2), 1–14.

Khanlou, N., Beiser, M., Cole, E., Freire, M., Hyman, I. & Murphy Kilbride, K. (2002, June). *Mental Health Promotion among Newcomer Female Youth: Post-Migration Experiences and Self-Esteem.* Ottawa: Status of Women Canada.

Khanlou, N. & Crawford, C. (2006). Post-migratory experiences of newcomer female youth: Self-esteem and identity development. *Journal of Immigrant and Minority Health, 8* (1), 45–56.

Kordich Hall, D. & Pearson, J. (2003, November). *Resilience—Giving Children the Skills to Bounce Back.* Toronto & Guelph: Reaching IN . . . Reaching OUT Project.

Landy, S., Masten, A.S. & Coatsworth, J.D. (1998). The development of competence in favorable and unfavorable environments: Lessons from research on successful children. *American Psychologist, 53* (2), 205–220.

Mental Health Association of Franklin County. (n.d.). *When a Parent Has a Mental Illness: From Risk to Resiliency: Protective Factors for Children.* Franklin County, OH: Author.

Miedzian, M. (1991). *Boys Will Be Boys: Breaking the Link between Masculinity and Violence.* New York: Anchor Books/Doubleday.

Millar, L. (2001, August). Boy—It's not easy being one. *Ontario Health Promotion E-Bulletin, 219.* Toronto: Centre for Health Promotion.

Millar, L. (2002, February). Little girls are made of . . . [Girls' self-esteem], *Bulletin 246.* Ontario Prevention Clearinghouse and The Health Communication Unit. Available: ohpe.ca/ebulletin/index.php?option=com_content&task=view&id=161&Itemid=78. Accessed on November 13, 2006.

Moeller, T.G. (2001). *Youth Aggression and Violence: A Psychological Approach.* Mahwah, NJ: Lawrence Erlbaum.

Mothercraft. (1999). *Growing Healthy Canadians: A Guide for Positive Child Development.* Sparrow Lake Alliance and Funders Alliance for Children, Youth and Families. Available: www.growinghealthkids.com. Accessed on November 13, 2006.

New South Wales Department of Community Services. (2003). *Discussion paper on the development of aggressive behaviour in children and young: Implications for social policy, service provision, and further research.* Ashfield, NSW: Author.

Ontario Prevention Clearing House. (2006). *Inclusion: Societies That Foster Belonging Improve Health.* Toronto: Author.

Pederson, P.B., Draguns, J.G., Lonner, W.J. & Trimble, J.E. (Eds.). (2002). *Counselling Across Cultures* (5th ed.). Thousand Oaks, CA: Sage.

Pendry, P. *Ethological Attachment Theory: A Great Idea in Personality?* Available: www.personalityresearch.org/papers/pendry.html. Accessed on November 13, 2006.

Pepler, D.J. & Craig, W. (1996). *A Developmental Profile of Risks for Aggressive Girls.* Unpublished manuscript. Toronto: York University.

Potegal, M. & Archer J. (2004). Sex differences in childhood anger and aggression. *Child and Adolescent Psychiatric Clinics of North America, 13,* 513–528.

Public Health Agency of Canada. (2004). *The Social Determinants of Health: An Overview of the Implications for Policy and the Role of the Health Sector.* Available: http://www.phac-aspc.gc.ca/ph-sp/phdd/overview_implications/01_overview.html. Accessed on February 27, 2007.

Quinsey, V.L., Skilling, T.A., Lalumiere, M.L. & Craig, W.M. (2004). *Juvenile Delinquency: Understanding Individual Differences*. Washington, DC: American Psychological Association.

Raphael, D. (1996). Determinants of health of North-American adolescents: Evolving definitions, recent findings, and proposed research agenda. *Journal of Adolescent Health, 19*, 6–16.

Registered Nurses Association of Ontario. (2002). *Enhancing Healthy Adolescent Development*. Toronto: Author.

Richard Weiler and Associates. (1994). *Youth Violence and Youth Gangs: Responding to Community Concerns*. Ottawa: Federation of Canadian Municipalities.

Rickert, V.J. & Weimann, C.M. (1998). Date rape among adolescents and young adults. *Journal of Pediatric and Adolescent Gynecology, 11*, 167–175.

Ross, L.E., Dennis, C., Robertson Blackmore, E., Stewart, D.E. (2005). *Postpartum Depression: A Guide for Front-Line Workers and Social Service Providers*. Toronto: Centre for Addiction and Mental Health.

Rutter, M. (1985). Resilience in the face of adversity: Protective factors and resistance to psychiatric disorder. *British Journal of Psychiatry, 147*, 598–611.

Rutter, M. (1993). Resilience: Some conceptual considerations. *Journal of Adolescent Health, 14*, 626–631.

Rutter, M. (1999). Resilience concepts and findings: Implications for family therapy. *Journal of Family Therapy, 21* (2), 119–144.

Sexton, T.L. & Alexander, J.F. (2000). Functional family therapy. *Juvenile Justice Bulletin*. Available: www.ncjrs.org/pdffiles1/ojjdp/184743.pdf. Accessed on November 13, 2006.

Skinner, W.J., O'Grady, C., Bartha, C. & Parker, C. (2004). *Concurrent Substance Use and Mental Health Disorders*. Toronto: Centre for Addiction and Mental Health.

Steinberg, L. (2001, March). *The role of the family in adolescent development: Preventing risk, promoting resilience*. Keynote presentation at the conference on Children, Youth and Families at Risk Program Initiative, San Diego.

Substance Abuse and Mental Health Services Administration. (1997). *Girl Power! Good Mental Health Is Powerful*. U.S. Department of Health and Human Services.

Ungerfeider, C. & Keating, D. (2002, November). *Education as a Determinant of Health*. Ottawa: Health Canada.

Waller, M.A. (2001). Resilience in ecosystemic context: Evolution of the concept. *American Journal of Orthopsychiatry, 71* (3), 290–297.

Walsh, F. (2003). Family resilience: A framework for clinical practice. *Family Process, 42*, 1–18.

Weikle, J.E. (1993). Self-talk & self-health. *ERIC Clearinghouse on Reading, English, and Communication Digest, 84*.

Willinsky, C. & Pape, B. (1997). *Mental Health Promotion*. Toronto: Canadian Mental Health Association.

Wolfe, D. (2003, November). *Tips for parents on building healthy relationships with their teenagers*. Press release. Toronto: Centre for Addiction and Mental Health.

Resources

Many useful resources are cited in "References" on page 91. Should you wish to find more information about building resilience in children and youth, you may find the following resources helpful as well. The Centre for Addiction and Mental Health publications are available by calling 416 595-6059 in Toronto or 1 800 661-1111 in continental North America.

Publications

Branden, N. (1995). *Six Pillars of Self-Esteem*. New York: Bantam Books.

Centre for Addiction and Mental Health. (2002) *Can I Catch It like a Cold? A Story to Help Children Understand a Parents' Depression*. Toronto: Author.

Centre for Addiction and Mental Health. (2005). *Wishes and Worries: A Story to Help Children Understand a Parent Who Drinks Too Much Alcohol*. Toronto: Author.

Coloroso, B. (2001). *Kids Are Worth It! Giving Your Child the Gift of Inner Discipline*, (rev. ed.). Toronto: Penguin.

Covey, S. (1998). *The 7 Habits of Highly Effective Teens*. New York: Fireside.

Deak, J. (2002). *Girls Will Be Girls: Raising Confident and Courageous Daughters.* New York: Hyperion.

Glennon, W. (2000). *200 Ways to Raise a Boy's Emotional Intelligence: An Indispensable Guide for Parents, Teachers & Other Concerned Caregivers.* Berkeley CA: Conari.

Greene, R.W. (1998). *The Explosive Child: A New Approach for Understanding and Parenting Easily Frustrated, Chronically Inflexible Children.* New York: HarperCollins.

Henderson, N., Benard, B. & Sharp-Light, N. (Eds.). (2000). *Schoolwide Approaches for Fostering Resiliency.* San Diego CA: Resiliency in Action.

Maisel, E. (2000). *20 Communication Tips for Families: A 30-Minute Guide to a Better Family Relationship.* Novato, CA: New World Library.

Manassis, C. (1996). *Keys to Parenting Your Anxious Child.* New York: Barron's Educational Series.

Seligman, M.E. (1995). *The Optimistic Child: A Proven Program to Safeguard Children against Depression and Build Lifelong Resilience.* Boston: Houghton Mifflin.

Websites

The Centre of Excellence for Youth Engagement
www.tgmag.ca

The International Resilience Project
www.resilienceproject.org/cmp_text

Public Health Agency of Canada: Mental Health
www.phac-aspc.gc.ca/mh-sm/index.html

Resiliency Canada
www.resiliencycanada.ca

Settlement.org: Newcomers' Guides to Education in Ontario
www.settlement.org/edguide

World Health Organization: Commission on Social Determinants of Health
www.who.int/social_determinants/en

Crisis line

Kids Help Phone
1 800 668-6868
www.kidshelp.sympatico.ca
A free 24-hour telephone support and information line for children and youth.